I0796796

Timothée Chalamet

Icon of our times

His life. his films. his style.

Carolyn McHugh

First published in the UK 2025 by Sona Books an imprint of Danann Media Publishing Ltd.

CAT NO: SON0630

Photography courtesy of

Getty images:

Steven Ferdman
James Devaney/GC Images
Gotham/GC Images
MEGA/GC Images
Stephane Cardinale - Corbis
Pascal Le Segretain
Marc Piasecki/WireImage
Christopher Polk/Golden Globes 2024
Gareth Cattermole
Michael Buckner/Variety/Penske Media
Michael Buckner/Deadline/Penske Media
Laurent Koffel/Gamma-Rapho
Darren Gerrish/WireImage
Paul Chinn/The San Francisco Chronicle
Emma McIntyre
Stefania D'Alessandro/WireImage
Jim Spellman/WireImage
Wendy Redfern/Redferns

Alamy images:

Featureflash Archive
TCD/Prod.DB
BFA
Everett Collection Inc
Abaca Press
Album
LANDMARK MEDIA
UPI
LMK MEDIA LTD
Maximum Film
Entertainment Pictures
FlixPix
Photo 12
Associated Press
Sipa US
Collection Christophel
dpa picture alliance
Moviestore Collection Ltd
Luke Sanderson

Other images Wiki Commons

Book design Darren Grice at Ctrl-d
Proof reader Cameron Thurlow
Editor Mathilde Pineau-Valencienne

Printed in the Dubai.

ISBN: 978-1-917259-04-0

Contents

A star is born

Chapter 1

Born and raised in the cultural heart of New York City, Timothée Hal Chalamet's path to stardom could seem almost predestined, given his artistic lineage.

He grew up in a family closely connected to the arts – his American mother Nicole is a former Broadway dancer from a family with strong ties to the film industry and his French father Marc is a successful journalist. His parents met in New York in the early 1980s and quickly bonded over their shared passion for the arts and for Marc's homeland of France. Nicole had studied French at Yale University, having spent time in Paris teaching English as a second language and also completing a master's degree in French literature at NYU. She even understood Marc's writing career, having also written 'behind the scenes' stories about show business for American newspapers including The Boston Herald.

The couple dated for several years before marrying in 1983. They waited again before starting their family, welcoming daughter Pauline in January 1992, then Timothée on 27 December 1995. Their parents' diverse and creative backgrounds significantly influenced Timothée and his sister, both of whose artistic talents were nurtured and encouraged from an early age. Even their neighbours were fellow artists as Timothée and Pauline grew up in the Manhattan Plaza building in the Hell's Kitchen district of New York, close to the theatre district. The Plaza's sought-after apartments provide subsidised housing and a supportive community for a vast range of performing artists with experience on and behind movie screens and theatre stages. Timothée spent his whole childhood in the building with his family, becoming well known to fellow residents. His maternal grandmother, also a one-time Broadway dancer, lived in the same building, five floors down.

Family Ties

Timothée's mother, Nicole Flender, is a native New Yorker with a background in performing arts. Her own parents also worked in the arts, her mother as a dancer and her father as a screenwriter, while her brother is a director, producer, writer, and actor.

Nicole began her career by studying ballet and performed with the New York City Ballet at the Lincoln Center as a child, before going on to train professionally at the Fiorello H. LaGuardia High School of Music & Art and Performing Arts. She went on to dance professionally on Broadway in musicals including *A Chorus Line, Fiddler on the Roof, Gypsy, Hello Dolly* and *My One and Only*.

Although she eventually transitioned to work in real estate, she has maintained her links with the arts through writing, her involvement with the Tony Awards as a voter and as an officer of the Actors' Equity Association.

She met Timothée's French-born father Marc Chalamet in the early 1980s when he was working in New York as a correspondent for Associated Press. He went on to found and run News of America – a news agency specialising in US coverage for the French-language press - until 2000 and has contributed news and features to a variety of radio stations and newspapers, including *Le Parisien*. His latest job is as an editor at UNICEF.

Meet the family....

Maternal grandfather

Screenwriter Harold Flender

Maternal grandmother

Broadway dancer Enid Flender

Maternal uncle

Director, actor, and producer Rodman Flender

Maternal aunt

Rodman Flender's wife, TV writer and producer Amy Lippman

Sister

Ballet dancer and actress Pauline Chalamet, who now lives in Paris. Like her brother, Pauline attended LaGuardia High School (she was in the Class of 2010) and went on to work as an actress in shows including *The Sex Lives of College Girls*, co-created by Mindy Kaling, and the 2020 comedy film *The King of Staten Island*. Timothée has described Pauline as his 'best friend'.

Pauline Chalamet

The family took full advantage of living in the bustling Big Apple and soaked in all it had to offer theatre-wise. 'I took them to see many different plays and musicals when they were growing up, and I think seeing certain performances influenced them,' Nicole said in an interview with the UK's *Guardian* newspaper. 'The productions they've seen, and even growing up in New York, has informed who they are today,' she said, remembering that Timothée's favourite was *Slava's Snowshow* for its magical production.

A clown performs onstage during a preview of the show *Slava's Snowshow*

Timothée was also riding the subway on his own from around the age of 10 – a native New Yorker with an independent character.

But summers were spent in France – specifically Chambon-sur-Lignon, in the Haute-Loire area, south of Lyon, where his paternal grandparents Roger and Jean lived. The French family influence was strong and Timothée and Pauline became bilingual, building up strong ties with their grandparents' country and developing a huge appreciation of French culture and customs.

NYC Subway train

Le Chambon-sur-Lignon tourist sign

But despite being steeped in show business, the young Timothée was more interested in playing football at first. He had a real passion for soccer, played competitively during his school years and is still an avid fan of French club AS Saint-Étienne, known as Les Verts.

Nevertheless it was perhaps natural that he would begin an acting career early, beginning with TV commercials.

He's said in interviews since that he didn't particularly enjoy that side of the profession, but it can't have put him off entirely as, aged 14, he went on to take up a place at New York's prestigious Fiorello H. LaGuardia High School of Music & Art and Performing Arts – the school on which the movie and TV show *Fame* was based. Renowned for its rigorous arts courses, LaGuardia's former pupils include Al Pacino, Jennifer Aniston, and Nicki Minaj. Timothée's mother and sister also studied there.

According to his drama teacher at LaGuardia, Harry Shifman, Timothée nearly didn't get into the school, which only takes an average of 40 students a year, selected from around some 500 applications.

'I remember his audition because I gave him the highest score I've ever given a kid auditioning', he said in an interview

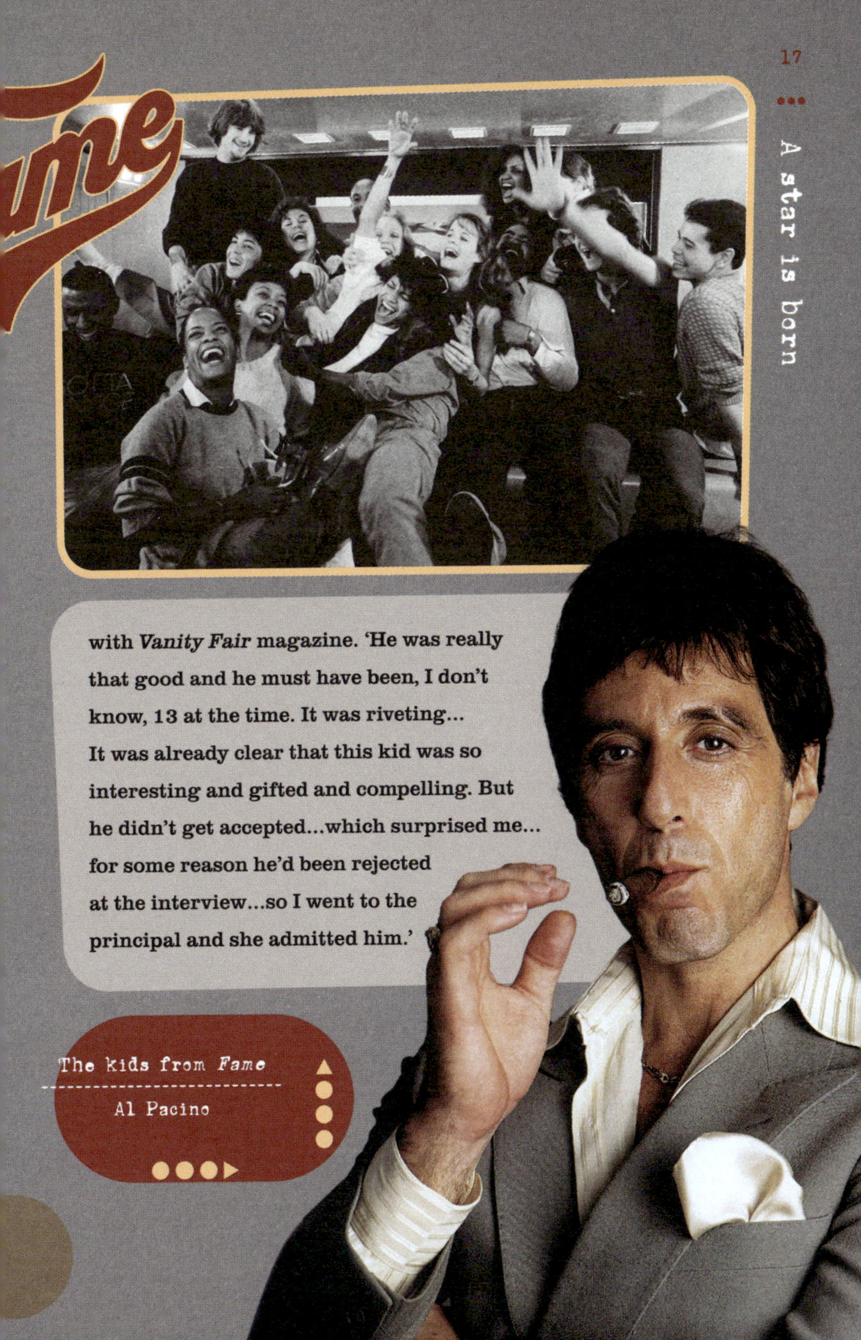

with *Vanity Fair* magazine. 'He was really that good and he must have been, I don't know, 13 at the time. It was riveting... It was already clear that this kid was so interesting and gifted and compelling. But he didn't get accepted...which surprised me... for some reason he'd been rejected at the interview...so I went to the principal and she admitted him.'

The kids from *Fame*

Al Pacino

Once in school Timothée worked hard and did well. Alongside comprehensive training in drama and performing arts, he took leading roles in several school productions, including playing Oscar in the musical *Sweet Charity* and the Emcee in *Cabaret*.

'There's a very famous scene [in Sweet Charity] where he's trapped in an elevator and I guess he's kind of claustrophobic,' continued Harry Shifman in his *Vanity Fair* piece. 'In my entire life, and I'm in my mid-sixties, I have never seen a more brilliant comic performance than Timmy gave in that scene. I think pretty much anybody who saw it would say so. People will eventually know he's an extremely gifted comic actor as well.'

Timmy with Caitlin Gann from the musical "Sweet Charity

But the competition was tough even in those early days – among Timothée's rivals for the best parts was school mate Ansel Elgort, a year his senior, who has gone on to find fame himself in movies including *The Fault in Our Stars*, *Baby Driver*, and the Spielberg musical *West Side Story*.

Poster for *Baby Driver*

Ansel Elgort

Early talent for performance

During high school Timothée made a music video 'Statistics' in character as rapper 'Lil' Timmy Tim. The video went viral when Timothée became famous and has since gained something of a cult following – partly because he references the probability of seeing himself on television.

He has talked about it in interviews since, describing it as a playful school project, and laughing about the fact that he still only got a D grade from his statistics teacher Ms Lawton, despite giving her multiple shout outs in the video.

'They [Ansel and Timothée] were both quite popular and very different,' said Shifman. 'They were both like rock stars in a way, in a school full of rock stars. Everybody recognised them as being particularly gifted.'

'It was an amazing creative and artistic school,' Timothée said in a 2017 interview with the *Los Angeles Times*. 'I struggled very much, leaving that place.'

But like all LaGuardia students, Timothée left the school when he was 18 and had to think about next steps. Perhaps not surprisingly his parents encouraged him to train for a backup career in case acting didn't work out for him. So he enrolled at Columbia University, majoring in cultural anthropology, but quickly realised that student life wasn't for him and that he was absolutely set on becoming a full-time actor.

So he transferred to New York University's Gallatin School of Individualised Study, where students are able to create their own study program of study. This meant he could pursue his acting career more flexibly.

He had no guarantees things would work out – but his inner voice kept encouraging him to have a go.

Columbia University Library

Gallatin School of Individualised Study

What's in a name?

With the French spelling of his name, Timothée should properly be pronounced as 'Tee-mo-tay' but he largely uses the English pronunciation – Timothy – and its diminutives Tim and Timmy. He has said in many interviews that he doesn't mind what he is called, as to insist on the French pronunciation 'is too obnoxious a requirement to put on people', 'pretentious' and 'unrelatable'.

Reflecting his popularity and the affection his fans have for him, he has several other sweet nicknames, including Timmy T, Timo, and even 'Tian Cha', which translates as 'Sweet Tea' in China.

Catching the acting bug

Timothée has often spoken of how much Heath Ledger's performance as the Joker in Christopher Nolan's 2008 Batman sequel *The Dark Knight* influenced his future career. 'When I was 12, I left the theatre, a changed man, after watching [it]. Ledger's performance inspired me, and I had the acting bug'.

Timothée Chalamet poses for a portrait to promote the film, "*Call Me By Your Name*",2017

Heath Ledger as the Joker

Early Days

Chapter 2

imothée began to add jobs to his acting CV from the age of 12, with what were fairly minor roles in commercials and TV shows.

He started out with appearances in the 2008 short films *Sweet Tooth* and *Clown*, while continuing to audition for more substantial roles. He had a minor role in the 2009 romantic drama television film *Loving Leah* and an episode of the TV show *Law and Order*, among other work. Then in 2012 his hard work paid off and he was cast in recurring roles on two major television shows, the medical drama *Royal Pains* (seasons three and four) and the Emmy-winning, spy thriller *Homeland,* starring Claire Danes and Damien Lewis (season two).

Playing Finn Walden, the Vice President's son, a charming but spoiled teenager in *Homeland* episodes which aired in 2012, he was included in the whole cast nomination for the Screen Actors Guild Award for Outstanding Performance by an Ensemble in a Drama Series in 2013.

While both these successful TV shows had helped establish him as a young actor to watch, his eyes remained on the main prize of a film role. So he was delighted to land his first part in a movie proper, when he was 18 and cast in the 2014 Jason Reitman comedy drama, *Men, Women and Children* - an examination of parenting and sex in the digital age. Featuring Adam Sandler and his LaGuardia schoolmate Ansel Elgort as part of the ensemble cast, it launched at the Toronto International Film Festival, but the buzz around it wasn't strong.

ark Feuerstein and Timothée
halamet in *Royal Pains*, 2009

Homeland, Season 2

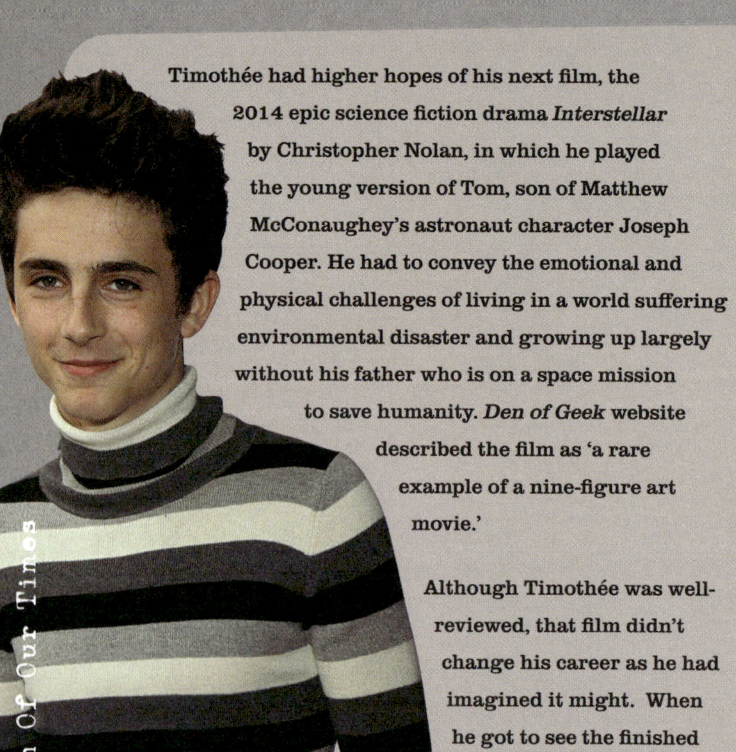

Timothée had higher hopes of his next film, the 2014 epic science fiction drama *Interstellar* by Christopher Nolan, in which he played the young version of Tom, son of Matthew McConaughey's astronaut character Joseph Cooper. He had to convey the emotional and physical challenges of living in a world suffering environmental disaster and growing up largely without his father who is on a space mission to save humanity. *Den of Geek* website described the film as 'a rare example of a nine-figure art movie.'

Although Timothée was well-reviewed, that film didn't change his career as he had imagined it might. When he got to see the finished movie he was dismayed to find that his screentime was more limited than he had imagined. Nothing had been cut, and he knew that his character was taken over by Casey Affleck for the scenes later in the movie when Tom had grown up. But nevertheless in his mind the part

Timothée Chalamet, 2014

was bigger than it seemed to be in the finished film and even his big monologue was heard rather than seen, as the camera was focussed (rightly as he noted) on Matthew McConaughey's reaction, with Timothée appearing briefly as a grainy image beamed to the astronaut from earth.

Interstellar poster

Christopher Nolan directs a scene from *Interstellar*

Speaking in the *Vanity Fair* 'Actors on Actors' slot in 2018, Timothée was keen to stress that he loved *Interstellar* so much that he went to see it a total of 12 times at the cinema and was very grateful for his part in it. 'It's always great to be working – I grew up in an actor's building in New York and I know the privilege of doing anything, [....commercials, whatever ...] to support yourself.'

But nevertheless he couldn't help being disappointed and said that he went home after the first screening and wept for hours.

Hopeful that *Interstellar* would be his big break he had dropped out of college and moved out of the family home to live in the Bronx – two decisions which he later described as 'presumptuous'.

No big roles followed and he remained the archetypal 'struggling actor'.

He also opened up in 'Actors on Actors' about how he had dealt with that disappointment, and others during his early career, including missing out after auditioning for Tim Burton's *Miss Peregrine's Home for Peculiar Children* and for the role of Spiderman which eventually went to Tom Holland when it was recast in 2015.

'I felt like I was getting close but I was so aware that the odds are always against you in the acting business. Nothing was happening,' he said.

Timothée Chalamet at the Los Angeles premiere of his movie *Interstellar* at the TCL Chinese Theatre, Hollywood

Movie Magic

Between 2014 and 2017 Timothée gained further experience of acting and film sets with roles in several movies including:

Worst Friends (2014)

This dark indie comedy featured Timothée as the young version of the adult lead character Sam. Although only a smaller role, it helped towards establishing him in indie circles.

One & Two (2015)

Timothy had a much bigger role in this story as Zac, one of two siblings with supernatural abilities who try to break free from their secluded and oppressive family life on a remote, mystical farm. He was critically praised for the emotional depth he brought to a character dealing with isolation and the desire for freedom, set against a mysterious backdrop combining elements of both fantasy and psychological drama.

*The Adderall Diaries (2015)**

This was another drama featuring Timothée as the younger version of the adult lead character. This time he was young Stephen, played as an adult by James Franco, in this memoir centred on author Stephen Elliot's struggles with a traumatic past and drug use as he becomes involved in a high-profile murder case. Again, although Timothée's actual screen time was limited, his portrayal of a 'troubled youth' was impactful and an important setup for the character's later issues with addiction and identity.

Love the Coopers (2015)

In this seasonal ensemble comedy, Timothée captured the awkward charm of his character Charlie, a teenager enjoying his first romance, set against a background of Christmas chaos and festive family reunions. The cast was led by comedy titans Steve Martin, Diane Keaton and John Goodman.

* NB this film was titled *True Deception* in some regions.

Miss Stevens (2016)

Timothée has described his role as Billy Mitman in the road trip drama *Miss Stevens* as the 'prelude' to his successful career proper. The film follows Miss Stevens (played by Lily Rabe), as she chaperones Billy and two other students on a road trip to a high school drama competition. Chalamet's character, Billy – a troubled but talented teenager - is a standout, especially during a climactic monologue he performs at the competition. This scene was important because as well as showing his character's vulnerability and depth, it allowed Timothée to give early notice of his own intense and introspective acting style and potential. He's said that he could entirely relate to the character of Billy as a kid who finds himself through drama.

Critics described his portrayal of Billy as complex and moving, and, along with audiences, found the monologue scene completely compelling in its rawness and honesty. The review site *Looper* ranked Timothée's performance in Miss Stevens as among his top five film performances, saying, '...the sense that Chalamet is on the very edge of superstardom is palpable in this film. Displaying the raw emotion that would soon earn him an Oscar nomination, this [monologue] scene almost feels like Chalamet's audition to become a major Hollywood contender, and it is easy to see from this performance that fame and recognition weren't far away.'

Timothée on Timothée

'[after Interstellar] ...I did more independent films and feel like that helped me not to be cynical and, in fact, to be inspired. I feel that [sometimes] people want a mirror in the things that they see. They want to see things shot in a way where they don't feel the sheen of Hollywood there. And they want to see stories that feel real.' Speaking in 2018 to *Vanity Fair's* 'Actors on Actors' feature.

VANITY FAIR

Again speaking in 'Actors on Actors', Timothée confessed that things got so tough after *Interstellar* that he had even questioned his career choice. 'That was the scariest year of my life. I didn't have a career, but I had tasted enough of the [movie] stuff that I could see what it maybe could be, but it wasn't presenting itself. I wasn't at school anymore and I had this complex, where I was like, oh my god am I one of those people that was happy at 16, 17, 18 and spends the rest of their life jaded?'

However he did have one highlight when he did some live theatre around that time, winning critical acclaim and the Lucille Lortel Award for Outstanding Lead Actor in a Play for the play *Prodigal Son* in 2016. But, other than that, nothing came close to giving him his first break. But all that changed when he won the role of Elio in *Call Me By Your Name*...

Clockwise from left, director Luca Guadagnino, actor Armie Hammer, actor Michael Stuhlbarg, Timothée Chalamet and editor Walter Fasano, to promote *"Call Me By Your Name"*, during the Sundance Film Festival 2017.

From Stage to Screen

Timothée's two professional theatrical roles were important in helping him develop and round out his acting skills.

Aged 16, and looking younger than his years, he played the 12-year old brother of the main protagonist in Anna Kerrigan's 2011 'coming of age' play *The Talls* at New York's Second Stage Theatre. He's said subsequently that it was the fun he had doing this play which made him realise he was ready to think seriously about an acting career.

He followed those stage appearances up in 2016 more notably when he took the lead role in John Patrick Shanley's autobiographical play, *Prodigal Son*.

His portrayal of the brilliant but troubled teenager Jim Quinn, a scholarship student at a New Hampshire boarding school – in a story based on Shanley's own experiences - was both raw and compelling. The story takes place over two years in the life of this problem child from the Bronx, who despite his academic abilities struggles with his behaviour which includes stealing, drinking, lying, and beating up younger schoolmates.

His performance earned him widespread acclaim and won him the Lucille Lortel Award for Outstanding Lead Actor in a Play.

In its review of the play *The Hollywood Reporter* described him as supplying 'a forceful presence' who 'plays the conflicted sides of Jim with raw conviction. He conveys the sharp, endlessly questioning mind and twitchy physicality of a tough kid who has come up in a brawling, blue-collar milieu and now feels awkward and defensive in an environment where self-discipline is considered the key to maturity.'

The New York Times described him as a 'real discovery' and said that he 'he fills a tall order of a character with enough easy charisma to confirm his status as a rising star.

'He is delightful when Jim pronounces the names of other people that he would like to have as his own: Rafael Sabatini (author of the swashbuckling "*Scaramouche*"), the poet Siegfried Sassoon or the gunman Elfego Baca. Savouring the grandeur of such nomenclature, Mr. Chalamet's Jim grows into a fleeting, flamboyant assurance'.

John Patrick Shanley, who also directed his play, appreciated Timothée's ability to bring depth and authenticity to the character, while *Vulture* said that it was a role he had been able to 'knock out of the park.'

Transitioning between stage and screen acting can be challenging as it requires a unique set of skills. Theatre acting often demands a heightened level of projection and physicality as actors have to convey emotions and character nuances to the entire audience, including those seated far away from the stage. In contrast, film acting relies on subtlety and precision, as the close up cameras capture every minute detail and expression.

Timothée's ability to navigate these differences so easily while still so young, says much about his skill and versatility as an actor.

In interviews, he has often reflected on the importance of his theatre background in shaping his approach to acting, emphasising the discipline and immediacy of theatre, which taught him to be fully present in each moment. He's been able to transfer this to his film performances, where his characters are often marked by a palpable sense of immediacy and authenticity.

Breakthrough

Chapter 3

fter teetering on the edge of stardom for several years, Timothée got his big break at last in the 2017 coming of age romance *Call Me by Your Name*.

His compelling performance as Elio Perlman, a 17-year-old who becomes swept up in a love affair with 24-year-old grad student Oliver, elevated him to international fame and movie heartthrob status. His subsequent nomination for an Academy Award for Best Actor fully established him among the most talented actors of his generation. Aged just 22, Timothée became the youngest nominee in that category since 1939 and the third youngest of all time.

This pivotal film in his career was an adaptation of a 2007 novel by André Aciman and follows the romantic relationship between Elio and Oliver which explores themes of first love, desire, and self-discovery.

The story is set over a few months in 1980s Italy where Oliver has joined the Perlman family as their guest during their summer break to assist Elio's father, an archaeology professor, with his research.

Asked to help Oliver settle in, Elio starts including him in his plans, introducing him to his friends, and taking him out for swims and bike rides. It is during this time that Elio starts to explore his sexuality and recognise that his developing feelings for Oliver go beyond friendship. When Oliver begins to respond, the pair embark on a secret love affair and develop a deep connection.

Timothée Chalamet and Armie Hammer in *Call Me by Your Name*

"A KNOCKOUT! CASTS A BEAUTIFULLY EROTIC, SENSUAL SPELL."
-Chris Nashawaty, ENTERTAINMENT WEEKLY

"RAVISHING FILMMAKING AND PIERCING WISDOM."
-Justin Chang, LOS ANGELES TIMES

"TIMOTHÉE CHALAMET AND ARMIE HAMMER SHOWCASE SOME OF THE RICHEST CHEMISTRY I'VE EVER WITNESSED IN A MOVIE. IT'S SUBLIME."
-Matthew Jacobs, HUFFINGTON POST

"SOME OF THE MOST EMOTIONAL MOMENTS IN FILM HISTORY."
-Tyler Coates, ESQUIRE

"★★★★★! TRIUMPHANT AND HEARTBREAKING."
(HIGHEST RATING) -Joshua Rothkopf, TIME OUT NEW YORK

CALL ME BY YOUR NAME

A FILM BY LUCA GUADAGNINO

All set against a beautiful Italian backdrop, the story shows the lovers exploring their identities and emotions.

The novel was a longtime favourite book of the director Luca Guadagnino, who personally chose Timothée to play the part of Elio.

In a 2018 interview with *GQ* magazine, Guadagnino explained why, saying, 'When I had lunch with Timothée for the first time, I immediately saw in his physicality the kind of feverish, nervous angularity that André described in the book,' he said. 'But most important, in conversation with Timothée, I learned that the young man was not only a veteran actor, having acted for many years already in TV, theatre, and even cinema, but he had the most intoxicating ambition to be a *great* actor.'

Luca Guadagnino & Timothée Chalamet during the Berlin International Film Festival 2017

US poster for *Call Me By Your Name*

This first impression was confirmed during Timothée's auditions for the part, which convinced Guadagnino, he had the perfect blend of intelligence, vulnerability, and charisma to carry off the complex role.

Guadagnino even went as far as to reimagine the character to incorporate Timothée's fluent French, which wasn't in the original novel. 'We made sure we could really use his Frenchness, the multilingual personality, and also his personality,' said Guadagnino.

But that's not to say the role was easy for Timothée. His character Elio was a precociously talented Jewish/French/Italian, so that he also had to learn to speak Italian and to play the guitar and the piano.

As usual Timothée took a deep dive into his preparations, arriving in Italy a full month and a half before filming began in May 2016 to give himself time to learn those skills, settle into the Italian vibe and fully embody the role. He was determined to make his portrayal of Elio authentic by ensuring he could convincingly perform the classical music pieces integral to Elio's character. This included working with Italian composer Roberto Solci and practicing daily.

He was already familiar with the novel, which he had read previously, describing it as 'a window into a young person'.

Filming took place in the idyllic countryside of Crema in Northern Italy, a sun-drenched summer setting that was the perfect back drop for the intimate and emotional story.

Timothée Chalamet and Armie Hammer in *Call Me by Your Name*

Timothée's nuanced performance perfectly captured the innocence and intensity of first love, drawing viewers into Elio's internal world.

While the whole film was a triumph for him, one of his most stunning scenes comes right at the end of the film, as the credits roll in what is a post-script to the main action. At the end of the summer, when Oliver's research job with Elio's father had finished, he and Elio had said goodbye. There is then a time hop to a future winter, as the Perlman family are preparing their Hanukkah celebrations, and Elio takes a call from Oliver saying that he has become engaged to a woman back in America. Clearly floored, Elio hangs up the phone and goes to sit by the fireplace staring into the flames. He is shown in close up as a range of expressions pass over his face while he allows his tears to flow, remembering the longing and love of their summer together. It's a four-minute-long scene, which Timothée filmed in one take. The camera was set in the fireplace with nobody behind it and the take was timed exactly to fit with the music, *Visions of Gideon* by Sufjan Stevens.

Discussing his former pupil once again, Timothée's former drama teacher Harry Shifman told *Vanity Fair*. 'He brought himself to that role and revealed all the many sides of himself. It was very courageous that he could do that. In that last shot – he has a marvellous ability to play opposite to what he's experiencing. So you see this inner dynamic pull between what he's feeling and what he's willing to reveal that he's feeling, which of course just provokes that emotion in the audience. That's very sophisticated.'

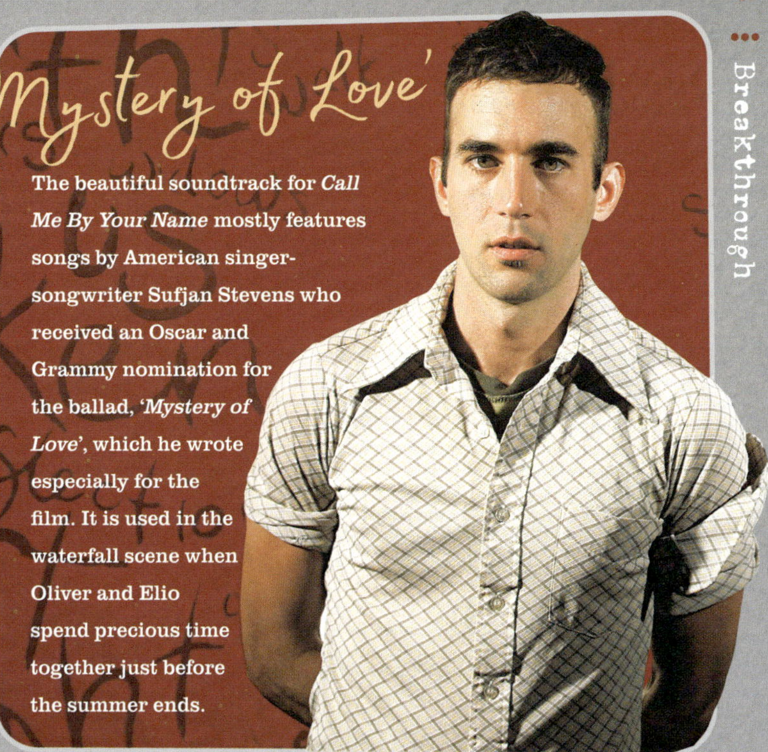

'Mystery of Love'

The beautiful soundtrack for *Call Me By Your Name* mostly features songs by American singer-songwriter Sufjan Stevens who received an Oscar and Grammy nomination for the ballad, *'Mystery of Love'*, which he wrote especially for the film. It is used in the waterfall scene when Oliver and Elio spend precious time together just before the summer ends.

Call Me by Your Name premiered at the prestigious Sundance Film Festival in January 2017, where it received a standing ovation. Among the critical acclaim came several references to Timothée's astounding ability to convey complex emotions with remarkable economy of dialogue. His subtle facial expressions and gestures became one of the film's hallmarks.

Critics were united in praise for his performance, with many highlighting his naturalistic portrayal of Elio's journey from adolescence to adulthood.

The Hollywood Reporter review hailed Timothée's performance as, 'the true breakout of the film.'

'The character of Elio feels like one that Chalamet was born to play,' agreed the *Looper* website, '... with the actor demonstrating his proficiency in music and languages in a way that is both utterly convincing and perfect for the prodigious teen he is portraying.'

The New York Times similarly loved his performance, noting, 'Timothée Chalamet is nothing short of extraordinary in his depiction of Elio, capturing every nuance of youthful longing and heartbreak.' *Variety* described his work as 'a stunning breakthrough,' while, in the UK, *The Guardian* emphasised his 'extraordinary ability to communicate emotion through the smallest of gestures.'

As well as the Oscar nod, Timothée's portrayal earned him over 40 more prizes and nominations during that year's awards season. He won the Independent Spirit Award for Best Male Lead and received nominations from the Golden Globes, BAFTA, and SAG Awards.

It was a defining moment in his career, a performance that continues to be celebrated for its emotional depth and authenticity. The film's exploration of love, identity, and the passage of time remains timeless, with Timothée's portrayal of Elio at its very heart.

Many commentators now consider *Call Me By Your Name* to be one of the best films of the 21st century.

Timothée Chalamet in *Call Me by Your Name*

Rising star power

Chapter 4

Movie Magic

Lady Bird (2017)

Lady Bird marked the writing and directorial debut of actress Greta Gerwig and was semi-autobiographical, covering her teenage years.

Although the film again covered a 'coming of age' theme, Timothée's role as Kyle, the love interest of Lady Bird played by Saoirse Ronan, was a world away from his part as sensitive Elio in *Call Me By Your Name*. Kyle was a bad boy with a huge ego whose character quirks and pretentiously over the top behaviour could have made him obnoxious. But as Timothée played him he was comical, and likeable enough to provide many of the laughs in this piece, which was billed as a 'dramedy'.

The film was highly acclaimed and nominated for five Oscars in the same year as *Call Me By Your Name*. As well as gaining plaudits for being involved in two Oscar-nominated films that year, Timothée made important connections with Greta, who chose him again a few years later for her 2019 production of *Little Women*, and co-star Saoirse who became a friend and also joined the Little Women cast.

Timothée Chalamet & Saoirse Ronan in *Lady Bird*

Greta Gerwig

Hostiles (2017)

Timothée's role in the 2017 film *Hostiles* marked another significant step in his burgeoning career. Directed by Scott Cooper, *Hostiles* is a Western set in 1892 towards the end of America's 'frontier' era when settlers moved westward across the country, often displacing native tribes.

Timothée took the role of Private Philippe DeJardin, a naïve and inexperienced young soldier in a military unit commanded by a Cavalry officer played by Christian Bale. Although not the focal point of the film, his part was recognised as contributing to the overall emotional depth of the story, with a review from *Collider* commending his performance as a testament to his versatility, and *The Hollywood Reporter's* review mentioning that although the part was small, Timothée had brought a necessary youthful presence to the ensemble, and managed to stand out among a strong cast including Rosamund Pike and Wes Studi, alongside Bale. He even got to use his French again as Philippe had a French accent, which naturally Timothée nailed perfectly.

Hot Summer Nights (2017)

Hot Summer Nights premiered at the South by Southwest (SXSW) Film Festival in March 2017 and received a limited theatrical release in the United States in July 2018.

Playing Daniel, an introverted and socially awkward teenager sent to live with his aunt after the death of his father, Timothée gave a multi-layered performance that anchored the film's dramatic arc. As he captured his character's evolution from innocence to reckless ambition after becoming involved with the local drugs trade, Timothée demonstrated his remarkable ability to inhabit vastly different characters convincingly. As well as solidifying his reputation as a talented young actor, this role also set the stage for his future success in Hollywood

Maika Monroe & Timothée Chalamet in *Hot Summer Nights*

Timothée Chalamet & Christian Bale in *Hostiles*

Timothée on Timothée

'I had a delusional dream in my early teenage years to have, in my late teenage years, an acting career... And in my late teenage years, working on *Homeland* and starting to do theatre in New York, I felt like I reduced my goal to something more realistic, which was to work in theatre and hopefully make enough money doing either a TV show or something I could sustain myself [with]. **And then it felt like every dream came true, exponentially. And then life is moving at six million miles per hour.**' Speaking to Vogue in 2022.

VOGUE

Although *Call Me By Your Name* – and the related Oscar nomination – first made the world sit up and take notice of this fresh-faced New Yorker, Timothée underlined his promise with two further films he'd made around the same time which also came out in 2017, *Lady Bird* and *Hostiles*.

Both films premiered at the Telluride Film Festival in September, then *Lady Bird* was released in the US on 3 November 2017, with *Hostiles* following in December.

Timothée Chalamet portrait, 2017

Now with critically acclaimed performances in three important films out around the same time – two of them Oscar nominated – Timothée entered 2018 as one of the most talked about young actors of his generation.

He was enjoying his first taste of stardom, but as he described the situation, his loss of anonymity was acceptable at that stage because the shift was undramatic. Speaking that year, he described the pride he felt in being in films that were super-successful, despite having relatively modest budgets. 'When I get stopped it's all about those movies,' he said. 'So it's not overpowering.'

So he happily stepped onto the whirlwind merry-go-round of promotional events that began with the film festivals of September 2017 and ran on to the lead up to the March 2018 Oscars ceremony. He was invited to thousands of functions over those six months, everything from screenings and award ceremonies to dinners, parties, and talk shows.

During that hectic time he built a reputation to be proud of on and off screen, proving that as well as being a supremely talented and acclaimed young actor, he was a popular, courteous, and entertaining guest. His awards season appearances, charming interviews, and humble yet charismatic personality captivated both audiences and the media.

And that's not to mentioning his new heartthrob status. Timothée's fan base was rising as fast as his career and this growing popularity was coined 'Chalamania'.

Timothée Chalamet
portrait, 2017

With his profile further elevated by his performance in *Beautiful Boy*, Timothée had solidified his status as a talented and serious actor and was now in demand for more high-profile projects.

The perfect vehicle came along when Greta Gerwig (who had directed him in *Lady Bird*) cast him as Laurie in her adaptation of the classic Louisa M. Alcott novel *Little Women*.

Laurie is the love interest of principal character Jo, played by Saoirse Ronan, also of *Lady Bird* fame.

Speaking via *The Hollywood Reporter*, Greta Gerwig said that Timothée's looks had played an integral role in his casting because she had wanted to explore the androgyny of the character.

'There's all this neat gender stuff about it, like Laurie is a boy with a girl's name and Jo is a girl with a boy's name', she said. 'I have them the whole movie swap clothing and they are each other's androgynous twin. [Timothée] was always the person to play this part for me because he has that – he's handsome but he's also beautiful. And Saoirse is beautiful, but she's also handsome. To me he was always the Laurie.'

US poster for *Little Women*

Kaitlyn Dever & Timothée Chalamet in *Beautiful Boy*, 2018

Critics agreed Timothée was a highlight of the film, bringing depth and charm to his part as he captured both the carefree spirit and underlying complexity of Laurie's personality, while managing to bring a modern sensitivity to the character.

Overall his performance fitted perfectly into Greta Gerwig's fresh take on the classic story, with his nuanced approach helping to showcase the multifaceted nature of Laurie's relationships with the March sisters, particularly with Jo and Amy.

The Independent newspaper praised his performance, noting that he imbues Laurie with 'the soul of a poet,' which makes his character's emotional journey more believable and relatable.

Empire magazine described his portrayal of Laurie as 'pitch perfect.' Its review mentioned his established chemistry with Saoirse Ronan, as bringing a modern energy to their interactions.

He was once again seen as a standout in an ensemble cast - no mean feat considering the other actors were lauded young talents including Emma Watson and Florence Pugh, as well as Saoirse, and more established Academy award-winning stars such as Meryl Streep, and Laura Dern.

Timothée Chalamet at the *Little Women* Premiere at Cinema Gaumont Marignan, 2019

Timothée Chalamet & Saoirse Ronan in *Little Women*

Timothée Chalamet in *The King*

It was becoming a theme. Ever since his first performance in Interstellar, alongside Best Actor Oscar award winner Matthew McConaughey, Timothée never seemed phased by the huge stature of his co-stars.

And in return these more experienced actors and actresses around him came to respect him and suspect he was destined for a big career. McConaughey himself offered Timothée advice and emphasised the importance of continuously improving and seizing opportunities. Back in those very early days of Timothée's career, McConaughey described him as having the potential to get better and better with each project, recognising his early achievements as a foundation for an illustrious career.

More recently, endorsement from his *Beautiful Boy* co-star Steve Carell reflected the broader sentiments swirling around the film industry regarding Chalamet's promising career prospects. Carell talked about Timothée's profound ability to tap into the emotional core of his characters, calling him 'a special talent' with a remarkable ability to bring authenticity and depth to his roles.

The industry was right. A leading role in *The King* in 2019 showed that he could lead a cast.

Then finally all the buzz around Timothée culminated in the huge achievement of being cast as a true Hollywood leading man. He was to carry the huge weight of expectations of not one, but two of the most highly anticipated films of the decade; *Dune* and *Wonka* ...

2018 Beautiful Boy

Timothée's role as Nic, a young man struggling with addiction in the 2018 film *Beautiful Boy* marked a significant chapter in his acting career, underscoring his ability to tackle deeply emotional and challenging roles. Directed by Felix van Groeningen, the film was an adaptation of two memoirs *Beautiful Boy: A Father's Journey Through His Son's Addiction* by David Sheff and *Tweak: Growing Up on Methamphetamines* by his son Nic Sheff.

Having caught the attention of producers and directors across Hollywood with his success so far, Timothée was an obvious contender for the part of Nic, which required immense emotional depth and vulnerability. But he still needed to audition. This was a starring role opposite the versatile and seasoned actor Steve Carell as David Sheff, and again, despite the differences in their age and experience, Timothée had great chemistry with the older, more experienced performer.

Timothée was keen to take on the part, both because it would challenge him and also bring awareness to the issue of addiction. In interviews he mentioned how moved he was by the Sheff family's story and the broader implications of the opioid crisis in America.

Conscious that he had a responsibility to depict the struggles of addiction authentically, he prepared extensively for the role, including spending time with the real Nic Sheff to understand his experiences and mindset.

Although he was well practised in playing troubled teenagers, there were additional pressures on this part, not least because he was playing a real person. Determined to do the story justice, Timothée lost 18lbs for the role, weight which he barely had to spare, saying that it helped him achieve an element of the disorientation and mania Nic would have felt.

'Playing a young person who's lost and self-loathing – that's universally relatable. I think it's the job of any actor to be as raw as possible and make yourself an open wound,' he said in an interview with *Time Out* magazine.

He did his 'job' well in a triumphant performance which was met with widespread critical acclaim for his authentic and sensitive portrayal of the painful realities of addiction. *The New York Times* highlighted his 'heart-wrenching performance' and noted how he 'beautifully captures the highs and lows of Nic's tumultuous journey.' Similarly, *Variety* described Chalamet's portrayal as 'brilliantly harrowing,' emphasising the emotional weight he brought to the role. Dan Jolin, for *Empire* magazine, described his performance as 'painfully convincing' and even compared him to a young Robert De Niro.

Among the numerous accolades and industry recognition he enjoyed on both sides of the Atlantic, came Golden Globe and BAFTA nominations for Best Actor in a Supporting Role. Additionally, *Beautiful Boy* helped to diversify his filmography, proving his capability in handling complex and mature themes.

US poster for *Beautiful Boy*

Timothée Chalamet & Steve Carell portrait to promote *Beautiful Boy*, 2018

Movie Magic

As Timothée grew in stature as an actor he took larger roles in bigger productions:

A Rainy Day in New York (2019)

In the role of Gatsby Welles, a wealthy young college student with thwarted plans for a romantic weekend with his girlfriend, played by Elle Fanning, Timothée gave an early hint of a future career in musicals in a scene where he sang 'I Can't Give You Anything But Love'. However despite complimentary reviews for Timothée's performance, the film had limited appeal and was shelved when allegations against its director Woody Allen resurfaced following the 'Me Too' movement .

Timothée Chalamet in *The King*

Timothée Chalamet in A *Rainy Day in New York*

The King (2019)

This was something different for Timothée – a lead role in a Netflix historical epic where he played against type and with an English accent as Hal, the Prince of Wales and future King Henry V of England.

In a big step away from the coming-of-age dramas with which he'd made his name, Timothée complete with unflattering 'bowl-cut' hair, charmed as the young prince unexpectedly burdened with the overwhelming responsibility of becoming King.

Critics agreed he was perfect for the role in this modernised and rewritten version of source material, including Shakespeare's plays *Henry IV, Part I* and *Part II*, and *Henry V*, bringing super-intensity to the part.

Little Women (2019)

Reunited with his Lady Bird co-star Saoirse Ronan and director Greta Gerwig, Timothée simply shone as Laurie, the charming neighbour of the March sisters, and Jo's love interest in *Little Women*.

In an interview discussing the film, director Greta Gerwig, who also wrote this adaptation of the classic story, praised Timothée's performance, highlighting his incredible chemistry with Saoirse Ronan. She described their dynamic as 'like combustion,' describing their appearances on screen as a 'bonfire' of energy. 'I think of them as my children... They are spectacular actors. I don't know how they do it, I mean it's magic,' she said.

For his part, Timothée told *Time Out* magazine that he would work with Greta, 'on anything' ... 'I'm just totally in awe of her. I like working with filmmakers who are ten times smarter than me'.

As one of the few key male characters in the story, and a literary heartthrob to boot, the part was challenging but one that Timothée made his own with another assured performance.

Rolling Stone's Peter Travers was among the many critics who commended Timothée's performance work, stating that his portrayal of Laurie was 'irresistibly charming'.

Little Women poster

Timothée Chalamet as Laurie

The French Dispatch (2021)

Having already put his French to effective use in *Call Me By Your Name* and *The King*, Timothée used his language skills again in Wes Anderson's movie *The French Dispatch*. Told in an anthology format, the comedy/drama film presents a series of different stories set in the 1960s in the satellite office of a magazine in a fictional French town.

In his story, 'Revisions to a Manifesto', Timothée got the chance to play comedy as Zeffirelli, a student activist who becomes the focus of an article written by journalist Lucinda Krementz, played by the Oscar, Emmy, and

Timothée Chalamet in *The French Dispatch*
Wes Anderson

Tony award-winning Frances McDormand. Given McDormand's veteran status, there was huge confidence in Timothée performance, as he acted with the conviction of someone who had been acting for a lot longer than he had. In a surprising romantic element to the story, the pair even embark upon a brief love affair and their chemistry was noted by critics.

Chalamet's performance in *The French Dispatch* received positive reviews, with critics praising his ability to bring depth and humour to his role. His chemistry with Frances McDormand, who plays the journalist Lucinda Krementz, was particularly noted.

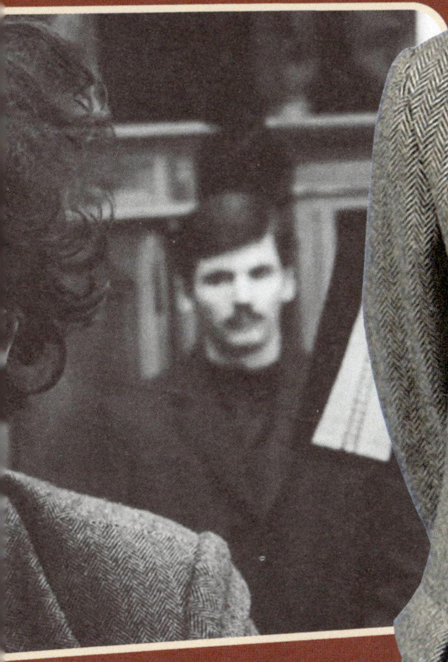

Navigating Super Stardom

Journeying through the sands of *Dune*

Chapter 5

Having earned professional respect for his acting and won the hearts of legions of fans, the stage was set for Timothée to take his first leading role in a major Hollywood blockbuster film.

But it wasn't just any leading role - the chosen project was out of this world as Timothée took the lead in the science fiction epic *Dune* – a highly anticipated adaptation of Frank Herbert's 896-page classic sci-fi novel of the same name. Written in 1965, the book is commonly regarded as one of the greatest science fiction novels of all time. Known for its complex themes, intricate plot, and richly detailed world-building, the novel has been adapted into several films, miniseries, and other media over the years and has a dedicated and loyal fan base.

As Paul Atreides, the young heir to the noble House Atreides, Timothée was cast through a combination of talent, timing, and the director's vision for the character. It was a key role as the story follows Paul's journey as he navigates political intrigue and conflict on the desert planet Arrakis, known for its 'spice', a highly valuable and rare substance with properties including the ability to extend human life and enhance mental capacity which make it the most valuable resource in the universe.

Timothée Chalamet promo artwork as Paul Atreides for *Dune*

Frank Herbert

Timothée Chalamet & Rebecca Ferguson in *Dune*

Director Denis Villeneuve

Director Denis Villeneuve, known for his meticulous casting process, saw Timothée as the ideal actor to bring the complex character of Paul to life. He had been impressed by Timothée's performances in *Call Me By Your Name* and *Beautiful Boy*, which showcased his ability to convey intense emotion and depth. Villeneuve said in interviews that Timothée possessed the rare combination of youthful innocence and mature wisdom required for the role, 'Timothée has this old soul in a young body, and that's what I needed for Paul Atreides'.

Then when Timothée read for the part he further impressed by demonstrated his deep understanding of the character. He said in subsequent interviews that he was determined to do the part justice on behalf of all the fans of the original Frank Herbert book because he imagined how he would feel watching one of his own childhood passions brought to life without due care and consideration for the source material. In preparation for the role, he immersed himself in the world of Dune, reading the novel multiple times, focusing on the philosophical and emotional layers of Paul Atreides, and working closely with Villeneuve to understand the director's vision and how to translate it to the screen.

In interviews, Timothée discussed the challenge and excitement of stepping into such an iconic role and talked about the importance of balancing the internal and external journeys of his character from sheltered young man to powerful leader. 'Playing Paul Atreides was about finding the humanity in this larger-than-life character,' he said.

He also underwent intense physical training so that he could cope with the physical demands of the role, which involved numerous action sequences, combat scenes and stunts. He spent months preparing for the shoot, engaging in fight choreography and strength training to ensure he could convincingly portray the young nobleman destined to become a messianic figure on the desert planet of Arrakis.

It was a significant step up in his career, moving from indie films and character-driven dramas to a behemoth production of grand size, scale, and scope, with a massive budget and huge global expectations attached to it.

Filmed in various locations including the deserts of Jordan and Abu Dhabi and featuring some of the biggest stars in Hollywood, *Dune* was such a monumental and breath-taking movie experience – from the set to the cast – that the key was not to get lost in such a huge production. 'The story was as I imagined, but the presentation was on a whole other level,' Timothy said about the project at the time. 'The films I've been doing are smaller.'

Admitting it had been a daunting undertaking, Timothée described it as like 'stepping into a machine or carnival that is already in motion'. Undoubtedly equipped to play this role, he nevertheless approached it modestly, saying in an interview with *Variety* that he felt a degree of 'imposter syndrome' alongside the big names in cast.

Denis Villeneuve and Timothée Chalamet filming a scene in *Dune*

Josh Brolin & Timothée Chalamet in *Dune*

But if anything this those feelings were helpful to him as an actor in capturing the multi-layered character of Paul Atreides, someone similarly 'burdened' by responsibilities and expectation.

And director Denis Villeneuve was unwavering in his belief in Timothée's ability to carry it off. '[He] is a very intellectual, very mature young man', he said. 'He has far more wisdom for his age than normal kids. At the same time, he looks very young. He sometimes looks like he's 14 in front of the camera. So it's the perfect combination.'

Critics and audiences agreed, with many reviewers highlighting his portrayal of Paul, with all its complexities and depth, as one of the film's standout elements. The *New York Times* described Chalamet as 'magnetic', commending his ability to convey the character's internal struggles and growth. *Variety* noted that Timothée brought a 'gravitas and intensity' to the role that grounded the film's expansive narrative .

With *Dune,* Timothée proved he was worthy of his status as a leading man in Hollywood able to carry a major motion picture. While he had already become famous by the time he was cast as Paul Atreides – with an Oscar nomination and a list of big films to his name – the outrageous success of the film and plaudits for his own performance brought him an even bigger audience than he might ever have dreamed about.

His portrayal of Paul Atreides is considered one of the defining roles of his career and his success with it bestowed upon him the almost magical power of being able to take his pick of roles – a quite staggering achievement for a 25-year-old.

Timothée on Timothée

I was grateful [for *Dune*]. The scale was *so* large, the actors were such titans. I felt a protected aura.'

Timothée Chalamet in *Dune*

Movie Magic

Dune (2021)

This epic film was widely acclaimed - particularly for its visuals, direction, and ensemble cast – with Timothée's performance frequently singled out in reviews as a key component of the overall critical and commercial success of the project. His ability to balance vulnerability and strength was seen as pivotal to making Paul Atreides a relatable and compelling character.

The Wrap described how director Denis Villeneuve's managed to balance the film's grand scale with intricate character development, particularly noting Timothée's portrayal of Paul as both a reluctant hero and a mystic figure.

Don't Look Up (2021)

Timothée appeared for only around four minutes in this Netflix comedy satire about a comet heading towards planet Earth, yet many critics felt he stole the show.

Playing well-intentioned but goofy skater, Yule, he was the love interest for Jennifer Lawrence's character during the impending end of the world.

The rest of the starry main cast included Meryl Streep and Leonardo DiCaprio.

Timothée Chalamet as Yule in *Don't Look Up*

Timothée Chalamet as Paul Atreides in *Dune*

Bones and All (2022)

Again working with *Call Me By Your Name* director Luca Guadagnino, Timothée starred in the genre-bending romance/horror film *Bones & All* in another surprising role, this time as a cannibal.

Timothée took the part of Lee, a drifter who along with his love interest Maren (Taylor Russell) is pushed to the margins of society.

It was a particularly challenging part, because as well as the tender moments in the story as Lee became vulnerable and fell in love with Maren, there were also some disturbing and visceral horror scenes during which Timothée needed to be scarily intense.

But nuance could almost be his middle name and he handled the delicate balance with ease, winning critical praise once again. The BFI's *Sight & Sound* film magazine described him as exuding an 'insolent confidence in his own beauty'.

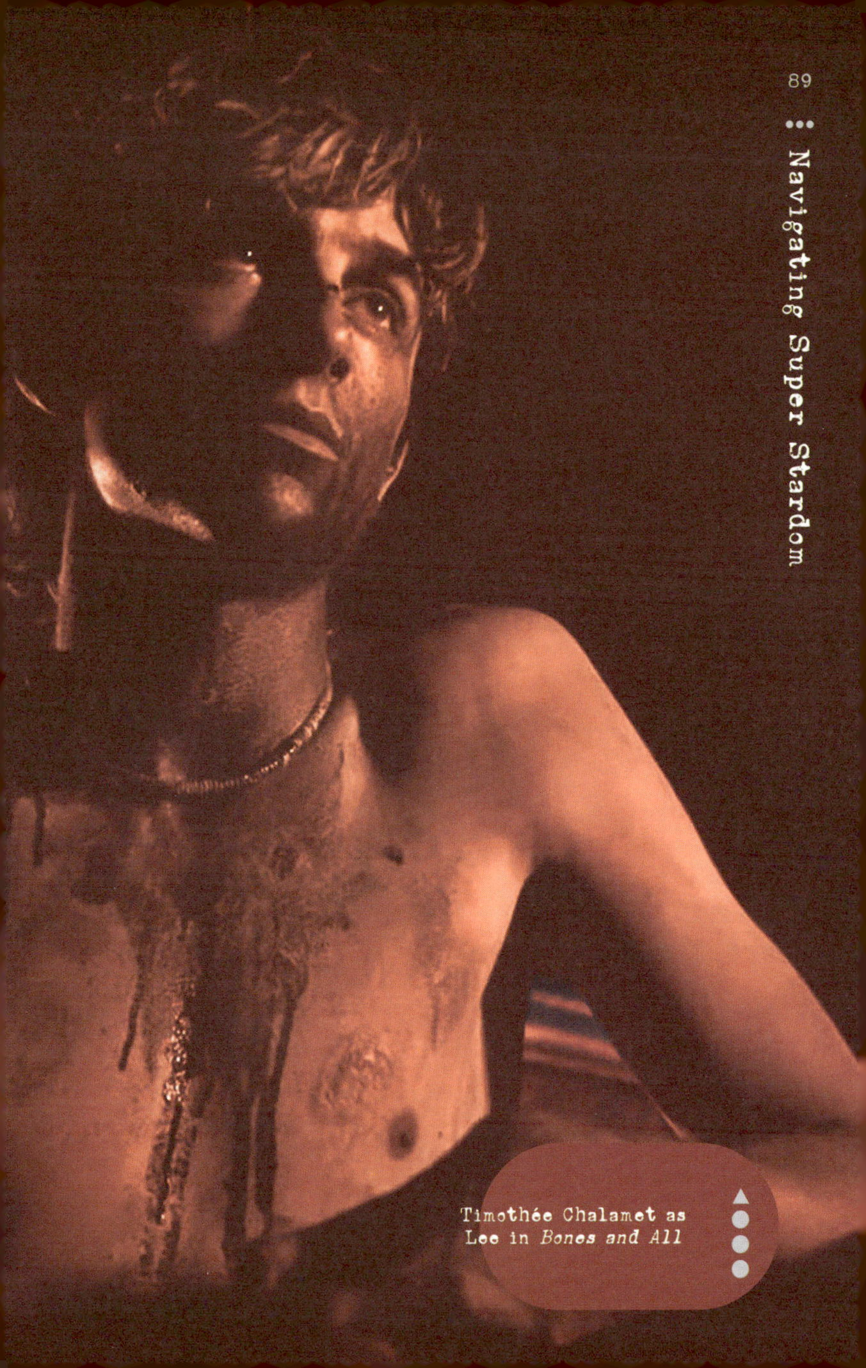

Timothée Chalamet as Lee in *Bones and All*

Timothée Chalamet as Lee in *Bones and All*

Timothée Chalamet as Lee and Taylor Russell as Maren in *Bones and All*

Becoming Wonka

Chapter 6

ow leading the pack of most sought-after actors of his generation, it shouldn't have been a surprise to anyone when Chalamet was cast as the lead in one of the most hotly anticipated big-budget movies scheduled for 2023.

And yet …

When news broke that Timothée Chalamet was to play the iconic Willy Wonka, singing and dancing in the musical *Wonka*, the excitement was simply off the scale.

Known for his serious, dramatic, and emotional roles, Chalamet's decision to take on a whimsical, fantastical character role was intriguing but also seemed risky. Eyebrows were raised. Critics were bemused. Many fans hadn't even known he had musical theatre training.

Yet the film's director Paul King, known for his work on the *Paddington* films, believed that Chalamet's versatility, combined with his inherent ability to balance charm with a hint of darkness made him perfect for the role.

He wanted a fresh take on the character for this film, an origin story, diving into Wonka's background. The story explored his childhood, the inspirations behind his inventions, and the key experiences that made him into the creative chocolatier created by Roald Dahl in his classic 1964 novel '*Charlie and the Chocolate Factory*'.

One of the official *Wonka* posters

Wonka bar detail from original book advert

Paddibgton Bear left.

For this prequel story, Wonka needed to be cheerful and full of optimism.

'When we first meet Willy Wonka in the movie, he hasn't really become the character that so many of us grew up with. But you feel there's so much joy, love, and kindness in him,' King told *Vanity Fair* magazine.

So the character of Wonka needed to be younger, more dynamic, and less cynical than the older man previously played on film, first in an iconic performance by Gene Wilder in 1971 and again in 2005 in a star turn by Johnny Depp. Those were big shoes to fill.

Chalamet, of course, did it perfectly, capturing the enigmatic nature of Willy Wonka while bringing new dimensions to the character that had not been explored before, such as naiveite, wonderment, optimism, and joy.

Timothée on Timothée

'I feel like early on in my career, I just wanted to work on things that were great, regardless of the size of the role. And it often meant working with a great director. I guess I'm trying to go where it's not obvious to go. And I feel *Wonka* is symptomatic of that'. Speaking to *Vogue* magazine in 2022.

VOGUE

Timothée Chalamet and the previous Willy *Wonkas*, Gene Wilder and Johnny Depp

Faced with the challenge of performing seven big musical numbers, Timothée applied his customary dedication and passion in preparation for the role. He took months of additional vocal training and attended choreography bootcamps to ensure his performance skills were as good as his acting. The intricate musical numbers alone required him to brush up his dance skills from his days back in theatre school and learn new styles such as tap and waltz.

'This was the most physically challenging project I've ever done," he told *Vanity Fair* at the movie's Los Angeles premiere.

'I can't say the singing and dancing comes easy. I've been around musical theatre my whole life, and danced a little bit

Timothée Chalamet in a scene with Hugh Grant as the original Oompa Loompa

in high school, but this was on a different level. It's different doing it on film. You've got to keep being in the centre of the frame while dancing, you've got to rehearse for months, you've got to be on for every take–take 12 and all the other takes–and dance with professional dancers ...So it was a big challenge.'

Timothée also had to interact with CGI and perform a flying sequence. The script was extremely complicated too, including complicated word play and tongue-twisting lines which had to be delivered at breakneck speed.

But the whole thing was a challenge he rose to with his usual flair. He gave it his all, never flippant while making the difficult role, which was the driving force of the movie, seem easy breezy.

When the film was released in 2023, his portrayal was roundly praised, with critics appreciating his fresh take on the character as he added youthful exuberance and a touch of melancholy to the role. He not only paid homage to the character's rich history but also brought a fresh, contemporary twist that resonated with both new and longtime fans.

Variety magazine described his performance as 'captivating' while *The Hollywood Reporter* considered that his 'magnetic screen presence', added a new layer of intrigue to Willy Wonka's fantastical world. *GQ* described him as an 'exceptional' Willy Wonka.

Wonka takes centre stage

Wonka was described by its makers as a 'companion piece' to the earlier versions of the *Charlie and the Chocolate Factory* films which centred on the story of Charlie Bucket as one of five 'golden-ticket' competition winners joining the quirky chocolatier Willy Wonka – played as fey, cynical and sarcastic – on a prize tour of his bizarre sweet factory.

But this 2023 film time puts Wonka, rather than Charlie, at the centre of the action and makes him the story's emotional heart. This new interpretation delighted fans and critics and grossed over $75 million domestically in its opening weekend, with a worldwide total surpassing $300 million within the first month of release.

Charlie Bucket from the 2005 *Charlie And The Chocolate Factory*

Timothée Chalamet in *Wonka*

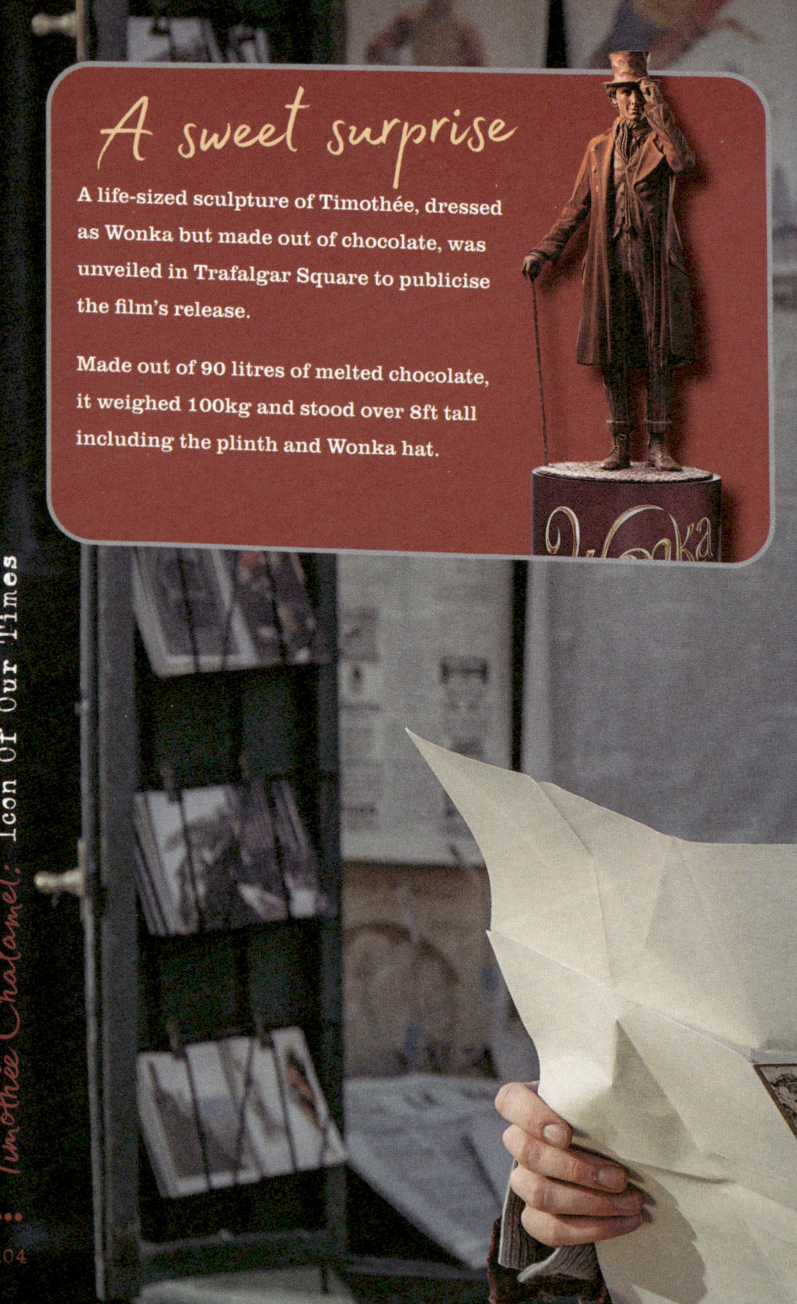

A sweet surprise

A life-sized sculpture of Timothée, dressed as Wonka but made out of chocolate, was unveiled in Trafalgar Square to publicise the film's release.

Made out of 90 litres of melted chocolate, it weighed 100kg and stood over 8ft tall including the plinth and Wonka hat.

kleine Ausgabe
Platze Reiseführer

Movie Magic

Dune: Part Two (2024)

For the second part of the Dune story – and concluding the adaptation of the novel which was always intended to be a multi-film project – Timothée reprised his role as the boy messiah Paul Atreides – and did not disappoint. He was joined again by the other main ensemble cast members Rebecca Ferguson, Josh Brolin, Stellan Skarsgård, Dave Bautista, Zendaya, Charlotte Rampling and Javier Bardem, along with new characters played by Austin Butler, Florence Pugh, Christopher Walken, and Léa Seydoux.

Timothée's character Paul Atreides remained central in this continuation of the Dune story, which director Denis Villeneuve described as being an 'epic war movie', adding that while the first film was more 'contemplative', the second would feature more action.

And for Timothée, as well as coping with the more physical aspects of the role, this time he also had the additional strand of a love story, between him and Chani, as they united to wage war on the forces that destroyed his family.

He and Villeneuve often spoke French to each other during filming. 'It was the way that we were able to find intimacy in the chaos. It was our protected landscape. A second secret language,' said Villeneuve.

The director said that he could see the positive changes which had happened to Timothée in the time between the first and second instalments of the movie.

'Six years older when he walked into the set of *Dune: Part Two*, and things were totally different. He was much more confident and his skills were much more solid,' Villeneuve told *The New York Times*.

A holistic approach to his craft

A holistic approach to his craft

Chapter 7

Timothée's preparation for his diverse roles is becoming legendary. Taking his natural talent as a given, it's this meticulous approach to his craft which has powered his meteoric rise in the film industry.

Known for the dedication and intensity he brings to each role, Timothée's preparation process is a blend of thorough research, emotional immersion, and, sometimes, a physical transformation.

He's discussed in interviews how he brings such a sense of authenticity to his roles by, firstly, researching the parts and the topics thoroughly. Then he will draw from personal experiences and emotions to find a genuine connection with his characters and immerse himself completely. For example, he has talked in interviews about his use of music to get into the right emotional state before shooting scenes. He also sometimes keeps a journal, as his character, to help him explore their thoughts and motivations more deeply.

While this is pretty much the textbook 'method acting' technique, it's an approach Timothée adopts with caution, as he wants to ensure that his focus remains on delivering an authentic performance, rather than becoming too consumed by 'preparations'.

In an interview with men's style and lifestyle magazine *VMAN*, he emphasised the importance of not getting too caught up in off-camera activities, which might distract from the on-camera

Timothée Chalamet featured *The French Dispatch* poster

Timothée on Timothée

'I do find that there's a fine balance between preparation and seeing what happens naturally'

performance. 'I try to be super careful,' he said. 'You don't want to be entertaining for the sake of being entertaining. The work should be the work. If it resonates, it's going to resonate, and then people are naturally curious about how you got to that destination. It can't be about how you're getting to it"

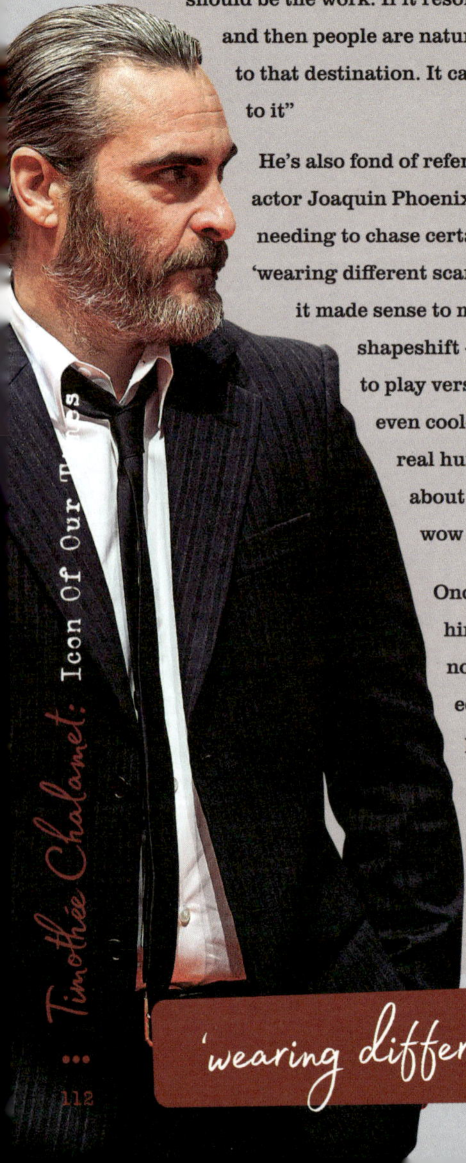

He's also fond of referencing something he heard actor Joaquin Phoenix had once said about actors needing to chase certain feelings, rather than 'wearing different scarves' ... 'and when I read that, it made sense to me...It's cool when an actor can shapeshift – and certainly you don't want to play versions of yourself – but what's even cooler is when an audience can see real humanity on screen and learn about themselves, rather than say, wow look at that guy go.'

Once on set, he likes to ground himself by looking around and noting surfaces, such as sharp edges, until he feels completely present.

Then beyond his own skills and talent, he is always eager to learn from others. He's said that he's taken small parts

'wearing different scarves'

Timothée Chalamet, 2023
Joaquin Phoenix
A holistic approach to his craft

Timothée Chalamet featured on *The French Dispatch* poster

in movies purely for the learning experience offered by being around acting veterans and greats. He mentioned taking the part in *Hostiles* mainly for the opportunity to play against Christian Bale.

He has also spoken about the importance of adaptability and the value of collaboration. He truly values the input and perspectives of his directors and co-stars, which he uses to fine-tune his performance.

As well as learning from his fellow actors, he has employed industry professionals where necessary to hone his dialect, movement, and vocal skills.

His reactions are as stunning as his acting. For example one of the most memorable scenes in *Call Me By Your Name* comes towards the end when Timothée's character Elio is sitting with his father who suggests that he knows about the love affair with Oliver and is sympathetic to his son's loss and hurt. Timothée is playing mostly in reaction as he listens to his father's apparent acceptance of his character's homosexuality. The whole scene is intense and made all the more electric by Timothée's expressions, stillness, and other non-verbal responses.

Timothée on Timothée

'I like to think that the need to act and be seen came from my mom's side, but the ability to *listen* came from my dad's side.' Speaking to *GQ* magazine in 2018

Insights and Plaudits

As these quotes and perspectives from Chalamet's directors, co-stars and collaborators clearly show, his success comes not just through his talent, but also because of his unwavering dedication to his art:

Luca Guadagnino

Director, *Call Me by Your Name:*

'Timothée is a fantastic actor. He has this almost unexplainable ability to convey the depths of his characters' emotions. He learned Italian, he learned how to play the piano, and he gave everything to this role. It's a rare quality.' (*Speaking to New York Times, 2017*).

Insights and Plaudits cont...

Scott Cooper

Director, *Hostiles*

'He's a very uninhibited actor... not afraid to take risks'. (*Speaking to Backstage 2017*).

Greta Gerwig

Writer/director, *Lady Bird & Little Women:*

'He's Christian Bale, Daniel Day-Lewis, Leonardo DiCaprio ...A heartthrob but with thoroughbred acting chops. Everyone else will be amazed by what he grows into, but I won't–I've always known that he's a unicorn.' *(Speaking to GQ magazine, 2018)*

Steve Carell

Co-star, *Beautiful Boy*:

'Timothée is an incredible actor. He has such depth and sensitivity to his performance. It's a challenging role, and he absolutely nailed it.' (*Speaking to Entertainment Weekly, October 2018*)

Nic Sheff

Journalist and recovering addict whose story is told in *Beautiful Boy:*

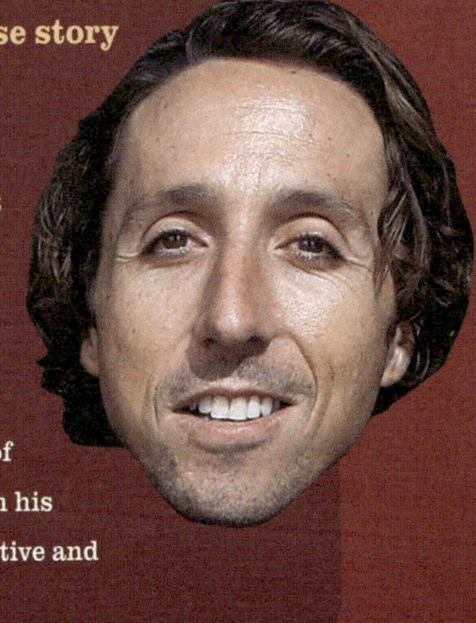

'I was immediately struck by what an incredible energy he [Timothée] has. But from the moment he sat down, I could tell that the only thing he cared about was making sure that he did this in the right way and portrayed this honestly and authentically. There's such depth to his person. There's wisdom, well beyond his years. He sort of flashes between being just a kid, having fun with his friends, to being this incredibly wise, contemplative and articulate spokesperson.'

Wes Anderson

Director, *The French Dispatch*

As tends to be the case with the directors who have worked with Timothée, Wes Anderson was full of praise for him, saying in a cover feature for *GQ* that Anderson 'knew [Chalamet] was exactly right' for the part of Zeffirelli when he was casting the film.

Denis Villeneuve

Director, *Dune* & *Dune: Part Two*:

'Timothée, we all know, is by far one of the best actors of his generation. And the thing is that I needed someone with that kind of huge talent who could sustain the movie on his shoulders, with all those skills. There's a lot of deep, deep, deep intelligence in the eyes, and he has an old soul. That was something I immediately realised when we talked with Timothée. Yet he looks so young on camera, for someone that seems to have a lot of experience.' *(Speaking to Den of Geek, September 2020)*

Zendaya

Co-star *Dune & Dune: Part Two:*

'He's obviously a very talented actor, but just a wonderful person and a good friend to have. Especially in this industry, it's nice to have other people who are going through it too and that you can talk to.' *(Speaking about Timothée to British Vogue in September 2021)*

Rebecca Ferguson

Co-star in *Dune & Dune: Part Two:*

'He [Timothée] brought the exquisiteness of art house [to Dune] creating another dynamic. He's phenomenal.'

James Mangold

Director, *A Complete Unknown*:

[Timothée has been] '...brave enough to stand out there and make himself vulnerable, throwing himself at this'.

A flair for fashion

Chapter 8

Beyond his acting fame, Timothée has become known as a razor-sharp fashionista, particularly on the red carpet where he has made some bold and eclectic style choices. *Vogue* magazine dubbed him 'the most influential man in fashion' and in October 2022 celebrated his achievements by featuring him as the first solo male cover star of *British Vogue* in its 106-year history.

His cover shot and accompanying interview highlighted his influential role in the fashion world as well as his reflections on his rapid rise to fame.

Now a seasoned leading man, his influence in fashion has grown along with his career, and he's become famous for blending high-end style with a fearless, experimental edge. His lithe, 5ft 10in frame makes him the perfect model for haute couture and off the peg alike.

Considering his stunning looks, fans were amazed to learn from a recent interview Timothée did with Zane Lowe for Apple Music that he had faced criticism of his slender appearance when he was starting out on his Hollywood career.

Timothée on Timothée

'Fashion is something that has always been so fun to me'.

Timothée Chalamet attends the *British Vogue* Celebrates Vogue Darlings party at Venice Film Festival, September 03, 2022

British Vogue, October 2022

Making headlines

Among Timothée's stand out looks...

A hint of his individualism came early in his carpet appearances when he wore a formal green blazer with a white t-shirt, black denim shorts, distressed trainers, and white ankle socks for the **premiere of *Snowpiercer* in 2014.**

He upped his game for the **2017 GQ Men of the Year party**, for which he wore a black and white gingham-look suit.

For the **2018 London premiere of *Beautiful Boy*** he chose a slim-fitting single breasted suit from McQueen's Autumn 2018 collection and wore a black V-neck tee and some fine necklaces. He accessorised with his favourite Chelsea boots, this time, a classic chiselled-toe version in black.

When Timothée attended the **2019 Golden Globes**, with his mum as his plus one, he wore a glitzy black sequinned harness with an embroidered bib from Louis Vuitton. Iridescent with black and purple beads, along with seven different shades of sequins, the harness reportedly featured a hidden pocket for his phone.

For a **2021 *Dune* photocall** Timothée wore what commentators described as a 'floral' Stella McCartney suit, but the pale blue and cream print actually featured mushrooms and was part of McCartney's Spring 2022 collection and made from 'zero-deforestation viscose'.

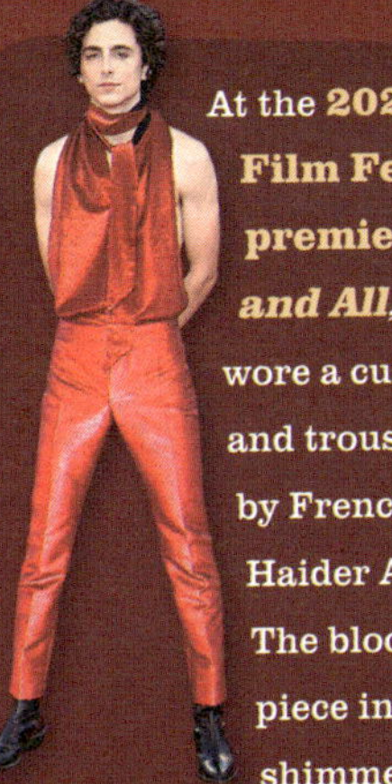

At the **2022 Venice Film Festival premiere of *Bones and All***, Timothée wore a custom made top and trousers designed by French/Colombian Haider Ackermann. The blood red two-piece included a shimmering backless halter top, with an attached scarf around the neck paired with matching fitted trousers.

Timothée's selection of outfits for the various ***Wonka* 2023 premieres** around the world were all carefully curated to pay homage to the film's 'sweetie' aesthetic in a trend the press called 'Wonkacore'.

In London Timothée glistened and gleamed in a single-breasted luxury leather, chocolate-coloured, crocodile-print, ombre Tom Ford suit. Then for Wonka in Tokyo he stayed with Tom Ford, but this time went to the other end of the colour and fabric spectrums, choosing a tuxedo in candy mauve velvet, which he wore with a Cartier necklace instead of a shirt.

'If I auditioned for *The Maze Runner* or *Divergent*, things of that variety that were popping when I was coming up, the feedback was always, 'Oh, you don't have the right body,' he said. 'I had an agent that called me and said, "You've got to put on weight," basically – not aggressively, but, you know.'

Overall his approach to fashion is notably gender-fluid as he mixes masculine and feminine styles, particularly through designers like Haider Ackermann, Louis Vuitton, Tom Ford, and Prada.

This willingness to step outside traditional menswear boundaries has sparked industry comment and conversations about gender fluidity and self-expression in fashion.

Where he does choose more classic menswear themes, he gives them a 'Chalamet twist' by selecting a particularly bold design or some off-centre styling.

Timothée on Timothée

'I hear about celebrities who have stylists, and that blows my mind. It's certainly not why I act, but I can wear cool clothes from some of the nicest designers in the world. So why am I going to pay someone to figure out what I should be wearing? That's the fun part.' Speaking to *Time Out* magazine in 2018.

timeOut

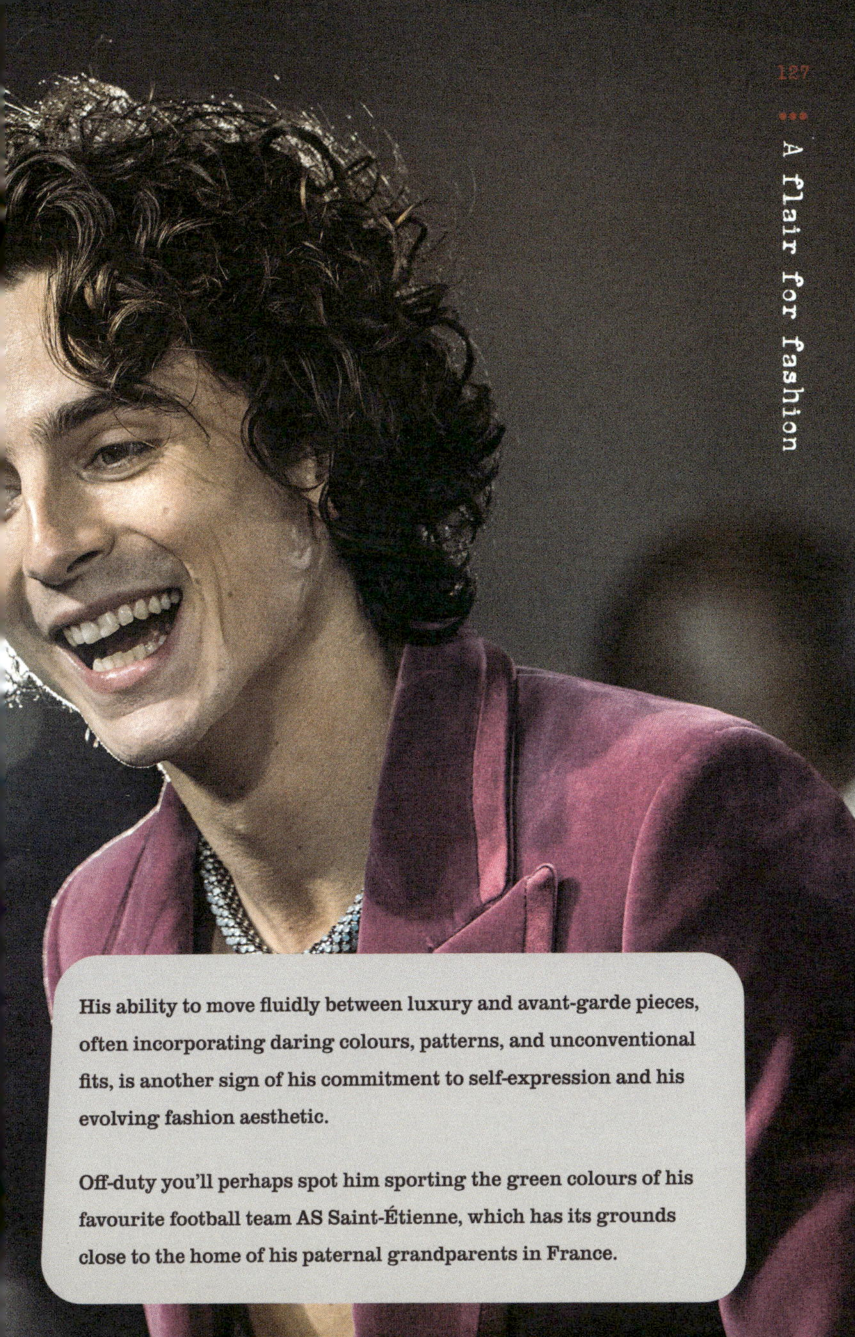

His ability to move fluidly between luxury and avant-garde pieces, often incorporating daring colours, patterns, and unconventional fits, is another sign of his commitment to self-expression and his evolving fashion aesthetic.

Off-duty you'll perhaps spot him sporting the green colours of his favourite football team AS Saint-Étienne, which has its grounds close to the home of his paternal grandparents in France.

His hair is also much admired by fans. When he lopped off his curls and adopted an historically accurate 'bowl cut' to play Henry V in *The King*, the 'Chalamaniacs' lamented the loss of his luscious locks. According to the film's hair and makeup designer Allessandro Bertolazzi, Timothée didn't love the look himself but wanted to be authentic. The short, cropped, bowl-style with shaved sides was popular during that period as a homage to monks and priests, and Henry V would certainly have reflected that fashion.

For those interested in seeing Timothée with other 'looks' there is even an Instagram account called @chalametinart that photoshops Timothée's face onto famous works of art – it has almost 60,000 followers.

Timothée has also been caught up in the internet's recent fascination with what are known as 'hot rodent boyfriends'.

As one Tik Toker put it 'Hot rodent boyfriend is, essentially, I want to say, like a hot guy, but he kind of looks like an insect. He's skinny, scrawny, a little weird looking, but hot, kind of grimy for lack of a better word, a little slick.' This group also includes Josh O'Connor, Mike Faist, Matty Healy, Barry Keoghan, Jeremy Allen White, and Glen Powell.

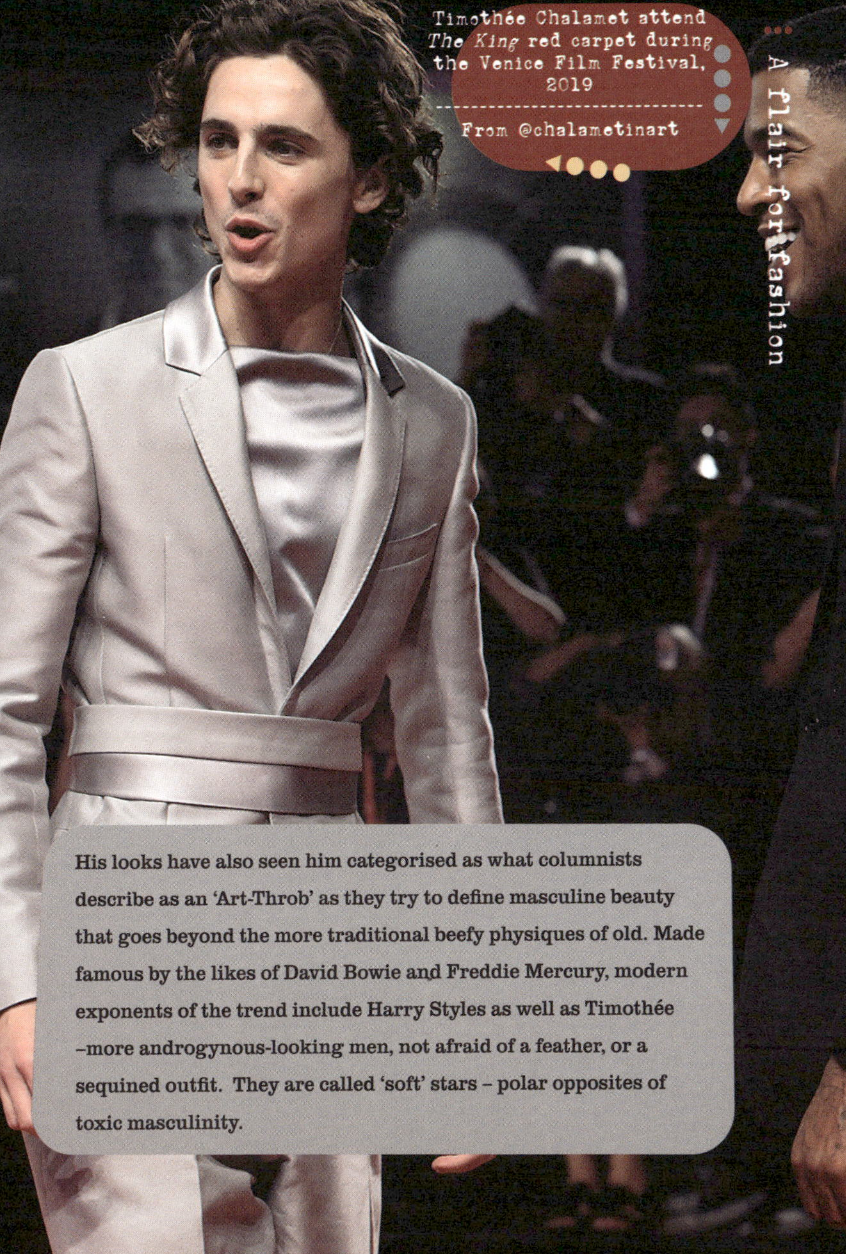

Timothée Chalamet attend *The King* red carpet during the Venice Film Festival, 2019

From @chalametinart

His looks have also seen him categorised as what columnists describe as an 'Art-Throb' as they try to define masculine beauty that goes beyond the more traditional beefy physiques of old. Made famous by the likes of David Bowie and Freddie Mercury, modern exponents of the trend include Harry Styles as well as Timothée –more androgynous-looking men, not afraid of a feather, or a sequined outfit. They are called 'soft' stars – polar opposites of toxic masculinity.

The man behind the fame

Chapter 9

As one of Hollywood's most-watched young actors, Timothée is under constant scrutiny and has to work hard to balance his professional status with staying grounded and maintaining a private life.

Known for being selective and thoughtful about public appearances, he has talked about the need to balance his professional life with meaningful personal experiences.

Emphasising that his personal life fuels his artistic work, he says it's 'essential to disappear' at times to preserve his inner life, which he believes brings depth to his performances.

Talking about his most recent project, playing Bob Dylan in the biopic *A Complete Unknown,* Timothée described his admiration for Dylan's ability to 'dodge' fame and maintain a sense of mystery.

Timothée Chalamet and Kylie Jenner at the 81st Golden Globe Awards held at the Beverly Hilton Hotel on January 7, 2024

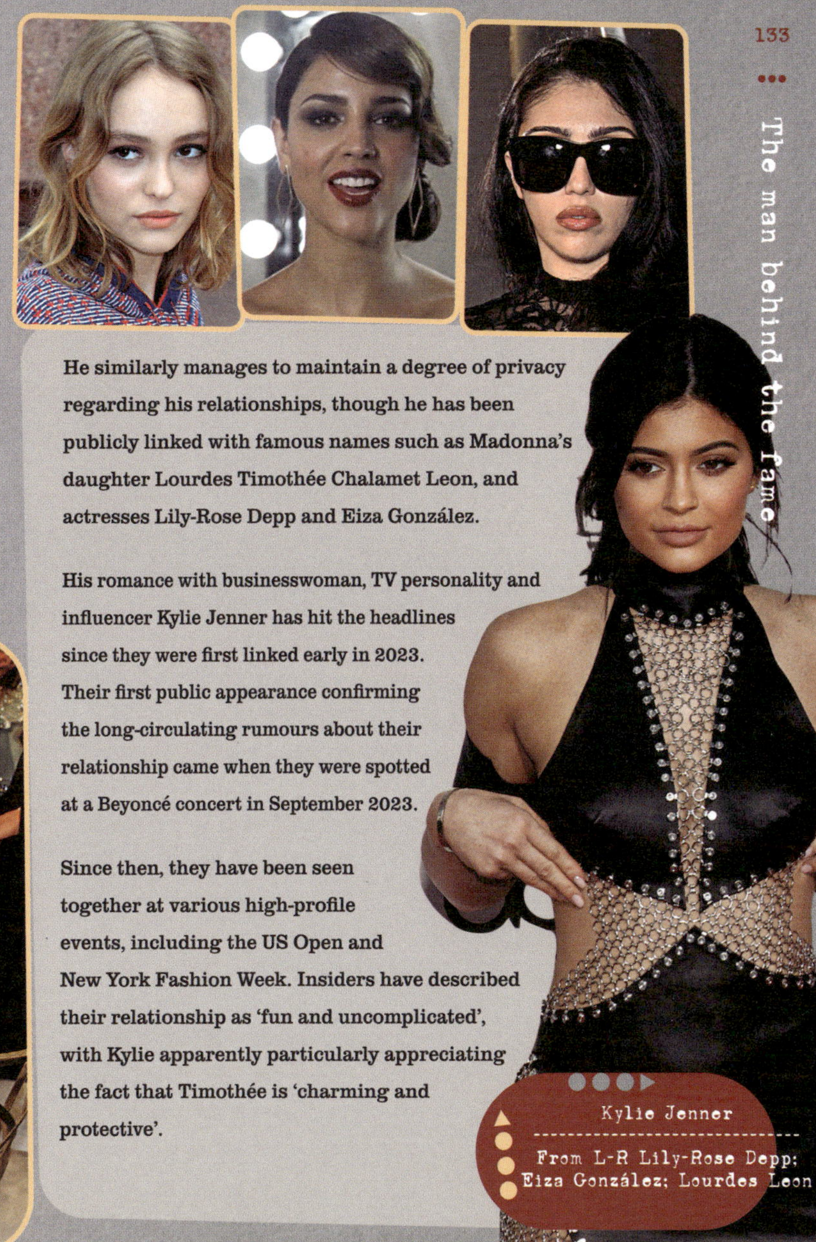

He similarly manages to maintain a degree of privacy regarding his relationships, though he has been publicly linked with famous names such as Madonna's daughter Lourdes Timothée Chalamet Leon, and actresses Lily-Rose Depp and Eiza González.

His romance with businesswoman, TV personality and influencer Kylie Jenner has hit the headlines since they were first linked early in 2023. Their first public appearance confirming the long-circulating rumours about their relationship came when they were spotted at a Beyoncé concert in September 2023.

Since then, they have been seen together at various high-profile events, including the US Open and New York Fashion Week. Insiders have described their relationship as 'fun and uncomplicated', with Kylie apparently particularly appreciating the fact that Timothée is 'charming and protective'.

Kylie Jenner

From L-R Lily-Rose Depp; Eiza González; Lourdes Leon

Despite the high-profile nature of their relationship, both have managed to keep most details under wraps, only appearing together at select public events. The media are naturally fascinated by their relationship not only because of their individual fame, but also because of the big contrast between their public personas.

While Timothée is barely visible outside his professional appearances and online, Kylie Jenner came to fame through her appearances on the reality TV show 'Keeping Up with the Kardashians' and leverages her extensive online presence working with high-profile brands as an entrepreneur and social media influencer.

However, despite all the column inches and intense media scrutiny he generates, Timothée manages to avoid discussing his romantic life, other than the occasional acknowledgment of the tension between public interest in his relationships and his desire to keep aspects of his life private.

Timothée Chalamet, his parents and his sister Pauline attending the 2018 Vanity Fair Oscar Party

Another topic beloved of journalists is about how 'French' he is. Although he has used his French language skills in a few films, he has never yet acted in a French movie, nor followed his sister Pauline and lived in France full-time. He speaks French when he promotes his films in France (media there describe him as 'Franco/American') and although his accent and fluency is pretty much flawless, he does revert to speaking English when conversations get complicated, which could boil down to lack of confidence rather than ability.

He remains close to his parents and sister, which might go some way to explaining how he stays grounded – even humble. Despite his incredible achievements he still seems to take on board that his success comes through working as part of a team. 'The role of an actor is never that consequential, even if you are making powerful work and people relate to it,' he told *The New York Times*.

Timothée loves...

ACTING - 'I'm not good at anything else' he jokes.

KID CUDI - American rapper and actor known for his 'new wave' of rap music has been listed by Timothée as an 'inspiration'.

BASKETBALL – He is a lifelong supporter of his home NBA team The New York Knicks

AS SAINT-ÉTIENNE – the French football team based close to his grandparents' home where he spent childhood summer holidays.

JUGGLING – one of his additional skills

International travel is a given for a modern film star and Timothée seems adaptable and comfortable wherever he works in the world and has to call home for a time. As a life-long New Yorker, he of course keeps a smart apartment in Manhattan. But according to *Homes & Gardens*, Timothée also now owns an US$11million home on the West Coast, in Beverly Hills, which he bought in 2022.

The house, built as part of a compound in 1976, was described by the magazine as 'refreshingly traditional' for an 'unconventional actor'.

The magazine described the 5,521 sq.ft. four-bedroom/five bathroom house as 'designed in classically New England coastal style' and featuring neutral décor, with light wooden floors, white panelled walls and ceilings, and plenty of windows to let in the Californian sunshine.

Extra features in the property's 1.55 acre grounds are a full-sized tennis court, a swimming pool and Jacuzzi and a guesthouse.

Previous owners of the house include supermodel Kate Upton and her baseball pro husband Justin Verlander, saxophonist Kenny G, tennis

legend Pete Sampras, and Hollywood producer Jon Peters.

Navigating fame also means carefully curating his public appearances. For example, after being announced as the new face of Chanel fragrance Bleu de Chanel in May 2023, he collaborated with Martin Scorsese on an ad for the fragrance that reflected humorously on his experience of celebrity life, blending his offbeat personality with a hint of self-parody.

Bleu de Chanel advert and Martin Scorsese, inset

From L-R Kate Upton and Justin Verlander; Kenny G; Pete Sampras

'In this short film, I'm playing sort of a caricature of what my life could be seen as, sort of in a hyper-realized setting, and sort of the publicity requirements that come with acting," he said in a behind-the-scenes video shared exclusively with *Harper's Bazaar*. 'One of the highest honours, if not *the* highest honour, of my career: to get to work with Martin Scorsese in New York. I'm a New York boy–I'm a New York actor. Checking something huge off [the] personal bucket list.'

Although outside of professional commitments he largely eschews social media, he does make some comments around news and current affairs.

Although admitting in an interview with *British Vogue* that he likes the immediacy, of some social media, '...there's a benefit to the TikTok generation that I feel like I'm a part of too: selfies and stuff, and the comfort with the camera...' he's not personally drawn to creating content. Despite that, he has 19.5 million followers and counting on Instagram.

He does occasionally advocate for social causes, such as Black Lives Matter.

And when allegations of historical sexual abuse by director Woody Allen resurfaced in 2018, in the wake of the Time's Up movement against sexual harassment, Timothée decided to give away his entire salary for his role in Allen's film *A Rainy Day in New York*. He donated his fee to three relevant charities – the Time's Up organisation, the LGBT Center in New York, and RAINN, (Rape, Abuse & Incest National Network) which is America's largest anti-sexual violence organisation. 'I want to be worthy of standing shoulder to shoulder with the brave artists who are fighting for all people to be treated with the respect and dignity they deserve,' he posted on Instagram.

Woody Allen

Timothée channeling Bob Dylan at the premiere of *A Complete Unknown* at the SVA Theatre on Friday, Dec. 13, 2024, in New York

Time's Up Movement:

Time's Up was launched on 1 January 2018, by over 300 women in Hollywood, including actresses, writers, directors, and other professionals, in response to revelations of sexual harassment and assault in the industry, notably those involving American film producer Harvey Weinstein.

While Time's Up also seeks to combat sexual harassment and assault, it has a broader focus on systemic issues such as workplace inequality, pay disparity, and the need for legal and policy reforms to protect workers in various industries.

This statement, issued early in his career, set the standards by which Timothée would come to be known. He's continued to be egalitarian, anti-discriminatory, polite, and humble – in short he's a modern-day gentleman.

He's always keen to credit the older actors who have helped and guided his career, from Matthew McConaughey who he met in 2014 on *Interstellar* through to his *Dune* co-stars Oscar Isaac, Josh Brolin and Jason Momoa, all of whom he has praised for their invaluable advice about navigating the intense pressures of fame.

Beyond these veterans, Timothée has found inspiration and camaraderie from a group of his starry contemporaries. He has been super-generous with his praise for his close friend and *Dune* co-star Zendaya and her boyfriend actor Tom Holland, describing them as 'good energy Hollywood'.

He has frequently praised Zendaya for her immense talent and inspiring qualities, describing her as 'one of the most inspiring people' he's encountered. 'Just how much she's able to achieve while also sort of letting everything roll off her back is mega inspiring, she's just doing.'

During interviews, Timothée has spoken highly of Zendaya's performance in *Euphoria*, calling her portrayal of Rue 'incredible' and 'insightful.'

Timothée has also spoken in glowing terms about his friendship with actress Florence Pugh – who he has worked with twice, firstly in *Little Women* and then more recently in *Dune: Part Two*.

Zendaya and Timothée Chalamet attend the *Dune: Part Two* Premiere at Le Grand Rex on February 12, 2024 in Paris, France

Keen to surround himself with people who, as he puts it, 'care about the right things' he is also good friends with fellow actor Austin Butler.

And of course he has always had a great relationship with Saoirse Ronan, another leading actress with whom he has worked several times. He has described their collaboration on *Lady Bird* and *Little Women* as 'formative' and expressed deep gratitude for their friendship. He admires her work ethic and natural rapport, stating that he's 'so ******* grateful' to work with her.

Their bond is one built on mutual respect and a shared passion for acting, with Timothée saying that he will even consider dedicating a chapter of any future memoir to her. For her part, Saoirse has praised Timothée's ability to keep her on her toes, saying ' I'm never quite sure what he's going to do next,' reflecting the dynamic energy they bring to their collaborations.

Will the real Timothée stand up?

Timothée showed his fun side – to the delight of Chalamaniacs, when he made a surprise appearance at a 'lookalike' competition in New York in October 2024.

Flanked by bodyguards, Timothée got into the centre of the competition before revealing himself to screams of disbelief as he briefly posed for a few photos with fans, several of whom were dressed in costume as his characters Willy Wonka and Paul Atreides.

Timothée Chalamet attends *A Complete Unknown* Contenders Screening at Museum of Modern Art on December 14, 2024 in New York City

The future

A Complete Unknown

Chapter 10

In the years since his breakthrough in *Call Me By Your Name,* Timothée Chalamet had become a Hollywood heavyweight. *Wonka* and *Dune: Part Two* were in the top five list of highest grossing domestic titles of the year. And while having two major films out just three months apart could leave an actor fearful of fatiguing fans, Timothée's audiences were happy with extra helpings of Chalamet.

Business Insider magazine declared that, discounting the Marvel franchise and animated releases, the last actor before Timothée to have two films gross US$200 million domestically so close together was John Travolta when *Saturday Night Fever* and *Grease* opened six months apart in 1978.

Timothée was not just hot, he was smokin'.

Early in 2024, on the back of those stunning box office returns, Timothée signed a multi-year feature film deal with Warner Brothers to collaborate on future projects both as a star and a producer. Rumoured to have earned more than US$8 million for Wonka, Timothée is now looking at double digit figures for his future leading roles.

He then set to work playing music legend Bob Dylan in an eagerly anticipated biopic called *A Complete Unknown*, starring alongside Elle Fanning and Edward Norton. The film is based on the book Dylan Goes Electric! by Elijah Wald which details the musician's early career, starting out in New York in 1961 when he was just 19 years old, with US$12 in his pocket and an acoustic guitar under his arm.

The story continues into the mid-1960s, during a pivotal time in Bob Dylan's career when things changed drastically for him as he rose to fame. It details his formative relationships with folk music stars including Woody Guthrie, played by Scoot McNairy, Joan Baez played by Monica Barbaro, Pete Seegar played by Edward Norton and Johnny Cash played by Boyd Holbrook. His co-star is Elle Fanning as Sylvie Russo, a composite character based on a few of Bob Dylan's real-life relationships, including Dylan's early 1960s girlfriend Suze Rotolo, who appeared on the cover of his 1963 album *The Freewheelin' Bob Dylan*.

The controversy when he shifted his style to electric rock is also covered, with a big scene set at the July 1965 Newport Folk Festival when Dylan shocked fans in one of the most famous moments in music history.

At the time, Dylan was a folk music icon, celebrated for his protest songs and acoustic performances. However, during his performance at the festival he took to the stage with an electric band, playing a set that included his most famous protest song 'Maggie's Farm' with amplified instruments.

Timothee Chalamet on the set of *A Complete Unknown*

TIMOTHÉE CHALAMET
as BOB DYLAN
EDWARD NORTON
ELLE FANNING
MONICA BARBARO
A FILM BY JAMES MANGOLD
A COMPLETE UNKNOWN
SCREENPLAY BY
JAMES MANGOLD
AND JAY COCKS
DIRECTED BY
JAMES MANGOLD
ONLY IN THEATERS
DECEMBER 25
SEARCHLIGHT
PICTURES

The response from the audience was divided, with a large number of fans expressing anger and disappointment, feeling betrayed by Dylan's departure from his folk roots. Many traditional folk music enthusiasts, including some prominent figures in the folk movement, were upset by his use of electric guitars, which they saw as disrespecting the purity of folk music. The jeers from the crowd were reportedly so loud that they could be heard over the performance and some of the audience even left the venue in protest. *Time* magazine described some fans as being simply overwhelmed by the 'ferocious shock' of the new sound.

The backlash was so intense that Dylan's manager, Albert Grossman, reportedly feared for Dylan's safety.

Timothee Chalamet on the set of *A Complete Unknown*

A Complete Unknown poster

But despite the controversy, Dylan's decision to embrace electric music marked a pivotal moment in his career, signalling his transition from folk to rock music and his adoption of new sounds. This set at Newport is now regarded as legendary – the turning point in his career, when he fully broke away from his folk music origins, changing both his own career and the landscape of popular music

Directed by James Mangold, Timothée plays guitar and sings live as he performs some of Dylan's most iconic songs in the film, including 'A Hard Rain's Gonna Fall'.

Nailing such a distinctive voice as Dylan's is a huge challenge and another example of the total commitment Timothée gives to his roles. He reportedly received guidance from Bob Dylan himself, who was actively involved in the film's development. James Mangold, who

Timothée on Timothée

'Leonardo DiCaprio said to me, "No superhero movies, no hard drugs" ...which I thought was very good - I follow them both! But the movie that made me want to act is a superhero movie, *The Dark Knight*. If the script was great, if the director was great, I'd have to consider it. *(Speaking to The New York Times)*

also made Oscar-winning 2005 Johnny Cash biopic *Walk the Line* – has emphasised the extensive preparation Chalamet underwent, including honing his musical skills over several years due to production delays caused by the worldwide Covid-19 pandemic and associated restrictions. As well as learning Dylan's songs and musical style, Timothée also immersed himself in the cultural climate of the 1960s. The 'being in New York' element came easily as many of the scenes were filmed in New Jersey, so Timothée was close to home.

James Mangold Timothee Chalamet on the set of *A Complete Unknown*

Timothée has described the process of playing Dylan as less about mimicking his exact mannerisms and more about capturing the essence of his influence and character. And according to James Mangold, the focus was on understanding Dylan's negotiation with his words and storytelling–qualities that define his voice beyond just the physical performance.

Although it's an interpretation rather than an impersonation, Timothée's vocals are utterly convincing. Of course *A Complete Unknown* isn't the first movie to feature Timothée's musical talents – he had seven song and dance numbers in Wonka. But this time he needs to put across a very well-known and instantly recognisable voice.

This is doubtless down to another strand of Timothée's preparation, deciding to work with the same team that helped his Dune co-star Austin Butler transform into Elvis Presley for the 2022 *Elvis* movie. This expert line-up included dialect coach Tim Monich, movement coach Polly Bennett and vocal coach Eric Vetro who is famous for working with Ariana Grande, Sabrina Carpenter, Shawn Mendes, Camila Cabello, Pink, and Katy Perry. He has also overseen vocals on more than 30 musical feature films..

Timothée has spoken of seeing Austin Butler's commitment to immersing himself in a role during the initial cast read-through for *Dune: Part Two*. Butler had finally dropped the Elvis drawl he hung onto long after filming finished but had already perfected the accent he needed for his *Dune* role as Feyd-Rautha Harkonnen, the son of Baron Vladimir Harkonnen, played by Swedish Stellan Skarsgård.

'I can't overstate how inspiring it was to me personally," Timothée told *GQ*, regarding Butler's ability to take his work so seriously. 'I just saw the way Butler committed to it all–and realised I needed to step it up," he said.

Timothee Chalamet and Austin Butler attend the *Dune: Part Two* Premiere at Le Grand Rex on February 12, 2024 in Paris, France

So what's next for this exciting young actor?

A third instalment of the Dune story, called *Dune Messiah*, is rumoured to be in development in which Timothée will reprise his role as Paul Atreides. Director Denis Villeneuve has said that he will wait a few years before starting the film so that Timothée is, and perhaps looks, older. That's because the story, based on the second Frank Herbert Dune novel, picks up the action 12 years after Paul's reign as Emperor of the Known Universe began and completes the character's arc.

Beyond that, it seems he will do whatever captures his interest. Whether portraying complex of young love, sci fi destiny or a pop legend, Timothée connects with his audience bringing depth and authenticity to his characters. He's leading the current pack of top young actors, shaping the future of cinema with diverse performances and contributions to both independent films and major studio projects.

His portrayal of masculinity – often described as 'softly masculine' – is very much on trend at the moment and is a quality that sets him apart in the traditional realm of Hollywood leading men.

Conveying strength through authenticity and emotional resonance, rather than physicality, Timothée puts the focus on vulnerability, introspection, and emotional depth. This defies conventional norms and is miles away from the archetypical 'tough-guy' portrayal often seen in mainstream films of old.

As *GQ* magazine put it, Timothée Chalamet is 'in possession of such preternatural talent that audiences start thinking about the actor's future not in years but in decades.'

There are evidently going to be many more chapters to write about the career of Timothée Chalamet ....

Filmography

Men, Women & Children **(2014)**

Interstellar **(2014)**

Worst Friends **(2014)**

One & Two **(2015)**

The Adderall Diaries **(2015)**

Love the Coopers **(2015)**

Miss Stevens **(2016)**

Call Me by Your Name **(2017)**

Lady Bird **(2017)**

Hostiles **(2017)**

Hot Summer Nights **(2017)**

Beautiful Boy **(2018)**

A Rainy Day in New York **(2019)**

The King **(2019)**

Little Women **(2019)**

The French Dispatch **(2021)**

Dune **(2021)**

Don't Look Up **(2021)**

Bones and All **(2022)**

Wonka **(2023)**

Dune: Part Two **(2024)**

A Complete Unknown **(2025)**

Marty Supreme **(2025)**

HOKA